The Bugman
on Bugs

Understanding Household Pests and the Environment

Richard "The Bugman" Fagerlund

and

Johnna Strange

Foreword by Governor Gary Johnson
NEW MEXICO, 1995–2002

UNIVERSITY OF NEW MEXICO PRESS ALBUQUERQUE

Library of Congress Cataloging-in-Publication Data

Fagerlund, Richard, 1943–

   The Bugman on bugs : understanding household pests and the environment /
Richard "Bugman" Fagerlund and Johnna Autumn Strange.

      p. cm.

   Includes index.

   ISBN 0-8263-3363-x (pbk.)

   1. Household pests.   2. Insect pests—Control.

I. Strange, Johnna, 1973–

II. Title.   TX325.F34 2004

   648'.7—dc22

                         2004003477

The Bugman on Bugs

Only after the last tree has been cut down,
only after the last river has been poisoned,
only after the last fish has been caught,
only then will you find that money cannot be eaten.

— Cree Indian Prophecy

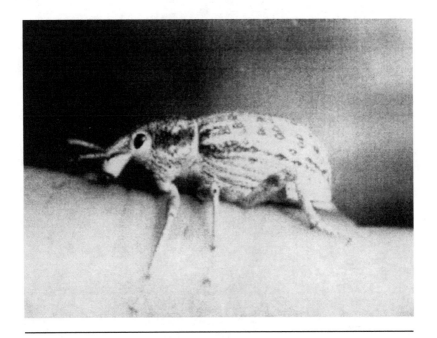

How can you not love this weevil? Wouldn't it make a great stuffed toy?

CONTENTS

FOREWORD

Richard Fagerlund and Johnna Strange have once again delivered a book that is equally entertaining and informative. In this book Mr. Fagerlund discusses the various types of common pests and the ways they are most typically exterminated. However, the problem, according to the "Bugman," is not the pest itself, but the pesticides used to exterminate them. Common pesticides have been proven extremely harmful, if not fatal, to animals and also to humans. There must be a stop to the unnecessary use of these dangerous chemicals.

Alternatives must also be given for what we use pesticides on. Cotton, for example, attracts nine different kinds of pests; as a result, twenty-nine different pesticides are sprayed. Cotton's alternative, hemp, only attracts two pests, whose removal does not require a pesticide. Hemp, if decriminalized, can help reduce the amount of pesticides deposited into the air, providing a safer environment for both humans and animals.

The Bugman on Bugs is more than just an encyclopedia on bugs and chemicals; it is a guide. By eliminating frequent misconceptions and replacing them with facts and proper procedures, Richard Fagerlund and Johnna Strange lead the way to a better, healthier planet, where pollution from pesticides is limited.

—Gary E. Johnson
Former Governor of New Mexico

ACKNOWLEDGMENTS

First I want to thank Johnna for agreeing to work on this book so soon after we finished the first one. Writing can be habit-forming, and hopefully we will continue to write. I want to thank a number of people for reviewing the manuscript as it progressed through various stages to finality. Katy Maddox, Beth Dennis, Rosemarie Romero, Greg Forbes, Joe Lally, Paul Chacho, Sandra Brantley, Rick Olcott, and Mary Bennett all read the manuscript in some form and made critical suggestions, most of which we adopted.

I want to thank all of the newspaper editors who run my column across the country and all of the readers who send me great questions and, very often, bugs to identify. If it weren't for the readers' interest in bugs and bug-related topics, this book wouldn't have been written.

Finally, Johnna and I want to thank Gary Johnson, former Governor of New Mexico, for reviewing the manuscript and writing the Foreword. Additionally we want to thank his assistant, Shannon Hickok, for her patience with my numerous emails and phone calls to the governor's office. Shannon was very pleasant to work with.

—Richard "The Bugman" Fagerlund

As I experience life, the peaks and valleys seem endless and sometimes treacherous. The past two years of my life have taken many turns and seem consumed by fire, leaving nothing but falling ash. Yet from that ash, life grows and another year comes to replenish what was lost with something new. These changes are never easy and I have been sent a few angels along the way to help me through. These souls I want to acknowledge with my deepest gratitude, for neither my art nor my words would have made it to this paper without them.

First and foremost, I would like to acknowledge my friend James Burroughs. I have never met a man with more integrity or genuine heart. His impact and influence on me has been immeasurable through his silent example. He helps me to believe in humanity despite all of humanity's flaws.

I would like to thank Geoff Mclellan for saving my life and giving me voice through song, Christen Smith Saam for being a wonderful friend, and all of my co-workers at Bound to be Read for all their support and love. I would also like to thank Konstantinos for being my Anubis through some of the darkest times of my life. I would like to especially express my gratitude to Nature, the Elements, and all living creatures for teaching me the most important of life's lessons.

Most importantly I want to acknowledge and express my love to my soul mate and husband, Andrew Davis Herman, and my two daughters, Audrey and Victoria.

My love I send to the World
May we love all life and not destroy it

Autumn leaves of beauty blanket the ground,
to prepare for the death of coming winter.
As the world seems frozen, the sun rises once more
only to bring another season of Life.

—Johnna (Autumn) Strange

INTRODUCTION

In the summer of 1973 I worked for a pest control company in Hollywood, Florida. We received a call to do a "cleanout" in a home in Ft. Lauderdale. I went to the house to render the treatment with a new employee who I was training.

When we arrived at the house and went inside, I knew we were in for an exciting morning as roaches and other bugs were running all over the place. The lady who lived there with her six children left. When we opened the kitchen cabinets, we discovered they were full of American cockroaches, lovingly referred to as "palmetto bugs" in Florida by people who don't want to acknowledge that they have cockroaches. We proceeded to fog the kitchen with a petroleum-based pyrethrum. The roaches came flying out of the cabinets and out from under the appliances and every other conceivable hiding place. We couldn't see the floor through the sea of cockroaches. There were so many that we couldn't stop them from running up our pants legs and crawling down our shirts.

We then went into the bedrooms and repeated the process of fogging and spraying. Large numbers of huge huntsman spiders came out from behind pictures on the wall, under furniture, and even under the mattress in the baby's crib. In the bathroom, a large, black scorpion came out of the overflow drain in the sink. In the paneled living room, the fogging drove out thousands of silverfish from behind the paneling, as well as hundreds of cockroaches and some more huntsman spiders. One spider affected by the fog mix was running across the ceiling when it fell and landed on my trainee's shoulder. He went screaming out the door, never to be seen again by our company. I don't think he even came back for his final check. The bugs were exiting the house through every possible area, including windows and doors. A neighbor who was watching began pouring a bag of chlordane dust along the property line to keep the bugs out of his house.

That was the most severe infestation I have ever seen in this business. I can only imagine what an adventure it must have been in that house to get up in the middle of the night and go to the bathroom or to get a glass of water!

WISDOM

This book is a sequel to *Ask the Bugman* that Johnna and I published in 2002. The subject matter of bugs, bug control, pesticides, Integrated Pest Management (IPM), and so forth, is so comprehensive that we couldn't cover all of the information in one book. The first book was based on my column that runs nationwide in many newspapers, magazines, and even online at www.hgtv.com. My column reaches more than seven million people. Because I get lots of mail every week, we decided to write this book to help people prevent and control the most common pests they encounter in their homes without using a lot of noxious pesticides or spending a lot of money on a pest control service.

Pest control is not rocket science. Anyone with common sense and average intelligence can control pests in his or her own home

---

Note that if you cover the right side of the face with your hand and then the left, you will find almost two completely different facial expressions. This face that I drew speaks for the soul and what it reflects in wisdom that is gained by experience. The lotus flower signifies the sacred spinning vortex blooming from the opening of the third eye. There are five dragonflies surrounding the face, and when connected in the circle would form a pentacle. The dragonflies to the left and right represent elements water and air, while the dragonflies at the base represent earth and fire. The dragonfly above the head represents the great Divine Source in which we are all connected. The choice of the dragonfly is due to its ancient nature and symbolism. Dragonflies can perform amazing aerial feats, imitating through their beauty and color how light can be directed. They are symbolic of joy. True happiness may only be found through experience that brings wisdom. Thus wisdom is gained when our experience returns us to a childlike state (innocence). The dragonfly represents this to me through play and evolution, for its life is spent in two realms—water and then air.

without using pesticides. Think about it, why do you even get pests? You probably invite them in. Not in the strict sense, but you allow conditions to exist that are conducive to pest problems. Almost every pest problem you develop can be avoided by employing a little common sense and a little knowledge. This book will give you the knowledge; hopefully you, the reader, are endowed with a generous amount of common sense (or you wouldn't have bought the book). As we go through the different pests in the book, we will tell you not only how to control them, but also how to avoid getting them in the first place. We will show you how to put out a "no vacancy" sign for the various pests in your area of the country. As a matter of fact, you will probably know more about bugs and pests and pest control when you finish this book than the average exterminator, unless he also reads the book.

Additionally we will explore other aspects of our arthropod neighbors. Arthropod, by the way, is a term given to all insects and their near relatives, such as spiders, mites, ticks, scorpions, centipedes, etc., and includes aquatic animals such as crabs and lobsters. All of these animals have "jointed legs," which is what the name "arthropod" means. There are other characteristics of arthropods, but there are plenty of books available for the person interested in the technical aspects of our little friends.

We will also talk about entomophobia, pesticides, bugs (arthropods) in spirituality and religion, bugs in poetry, bugs in folklore, and other aspects of these interesting animals. Additionally we will discuss why we need to have respect for all wildlife and why we should not tolerate the indiscriminate killing or abuse of any living creature.

All photos in this book are by the authors. All line drawings are in the public domain. All other graphics are courtesy Clip Art ©1990–97, RT Computer Graphics, Inc., NM.

1. ENTOMOPHOBIA

*I think I could turn, and live with animals, they are so placid
  and self-contain'd
I stand and look at them long and long*

*They do not sweat and whine about their conditions,
They do not lie awake in the dark and weep for their sins,
They do not make me sick discussing their duty to God,
Not one is dissatisfied, not one is demented with the mania of
  owning things,
Not one kneels to another, nor to his kind that lived thousands
  of years ago,
Not one is respectable or unhappy over the whole earth.*

—Walt Whitman,
from section 32 of *Leaves of Grass*

One day when I was pulling into my driveway, my cell phone rang. It was my daughter Sara. I walked into the house and found her standing on the couch, trying to call me and screaming at the same time. She pointed to a large wolf spider on the floor that appeared to be running around in circles. When I asked her what happened, she said the spider came out of nowhere and attacked her, and she had to defend herself with a can of aerosol cooking oil. The poor spider had the oil in its eight little eyes and couldn't see where it was going; thus it was running around in circles. I picked the spider up and put it outside where it could try to clear its vision without getting stepped on.

My daughter has always had a mortal fear of bugs, and I never knew why. I always had lots of bugs around the house, and I certainly never taught her to be afraid of them, but she has had, and still has, this fear. One time when she was dancing (she was an ecdysiast [stripper]), a cockroach ran across the stage, causing her to panic, fall off the stage, and sprain her hand. She wouldn't go back to work until the manager sprayed the building for roaches.

The fear of bugs is called "entomophobia" and this condition affects a lot of people. It isn't known what causes entomophobia, but I think you can rule out it being hereditary. My late wife was no more afraid of bugs then I am.

Most people do not like having insects and spiders in their homes or workplaces, and some may express fear simply being around them or seeing them. Fear is a reasonable and appropriate response to situations that involve potential danger, and many people consider all bugs dangerous. However, a persistent, irrational, and disproportionate fear in most situations where there isn't any danger is a phobia (from the Greek *phobos*, meaning terror). In extreme cases this phobia can become extremely debilitating.

I was deathly afraid of spiders (arachnophobia) when I was growing up. It wasn't until I got into the pest control business over thirty years ago that I forced myself to overcome this fear. The first time I had to go under a house to look for termites and I crawled through some spiderwebs I thought I would die. I knew I had to get over my fears if I was going to stay in the bug business. I learned everything I could about the potential "enemy" until I realized my fears were in my head and not at all reasonable. Now I have no problem crawling around under a house with thousands of spiders. In fact, spiders are very common in my house.

Behavior therapy, similar to what I did, is the most commonly recommended course of treatment for simple phobias and is based on the thesis that phobias are a learned condition and that they can be unlearned. Therapy includes a series of desensitization techniques that rely on increasing physical exposure to insects or spiders that cause the phobia. The goal is to systematically reduce the level of fear, but it may never be completely eliminated. In my case, I have completely eliminated my fear of spiders. I have not, however, been able to conquer my fear of heights, and to this day, I still do not climb ladders.

Of all the bug calls I get, the ones that are the most frustrating are from people who suffer from Delusory Parasitosis (DP). Delusory Parasitosis is a condition where someone feels insects, mites, or worms crawling on them. Usually by the time they call me they have already been to several doctors who tell them they have a rash caused by an unknown agent, or they have talked to some pest control companies that recommended spraying the home, even without knowing for sure what the pest is.

People who suffer from DP often go to extraordinary methods to rid themselves the "bugs." One fellow actually bathed in lindane, a chlorinated hydrocarbon, and then sprayed himself with Dursban. Other people have used a variety of other caustic chemicals in an attempt to get relief from the "bugs."

There are many non-arthropod agents that cause DP. Dry, sensitive skin is very susceptible to these crawling sensations. "Bites" can be the result of static electricity interacting with small particles such as paper, metal, and fiberglass fragments. Fibers from new carpets may be attracted to lower portions of the body because of static electricity, and these can be mistaken for bites. Electronic equipment such as office equipment or computer components can generate an electrostatic charge, which can also be problematic.

DP can result from physiological causes such as allergies, nutritional deficiencies, drug reactions, and other medical conditions. Materials such as detergents, fabric softeners, shampoo, lotions, insect repellents, deodorants, and almost any other substance that contacts the skin can cause skin allergies. These allergies can be mistaken for insect activity.

Drugs, which are prescribed for the elderly for a variety of ailments, are particularly likely to cause side effects that could result in symptoms similar to DP. Drugs are not limited to prescribed forms. Recreational drugs like marijuana, cocaine, LSD, and methamphetamines can cause symptoms that will make people believe they are "infested" with bugs.

DP can be triggered by psychological problems as well. Symptoms of anxiety, stress, tension, depression, and fatigue can manifest themselves as itching or tingling. Some cases involve lonely people who need interactions with other humans. The power of suggestion is also a factor in DP. People who are around folks with DP will often find themselves scratching, which explains

TRANSFORMATION

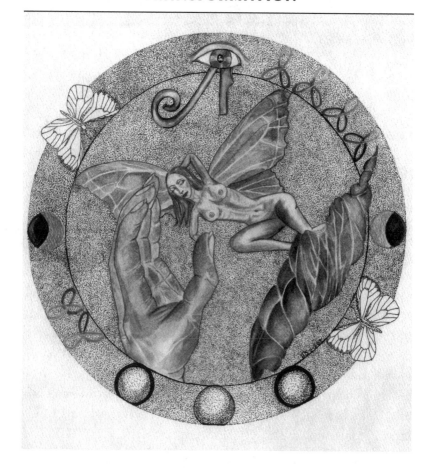

why a couple of people in the household may get the condition while others will not.

Are there any situations where "bugs" are responsible? Yes, typical culprits include thrips brought in on flowers, bird or rodent mites from nests in or on the building, or parasites such as bed bugs, lice, or fleas. A competent pest control professional or entomologist upon inspection of the patient's home can find these arthropods. If insects and mites are not found, then DP has to be considered a real possibility. I have a standard statement I issue when I am dealing with DP patients. "Although I found no insects or mites in the samples you provided, the symptoms you are experiencing are real and deserve further investigation." The idea is to get the DP sufferer to see a physician and receive the appropriate health care.

Transformation is symbolic of the metamorphic stages of change, as with the butterfly and moth. This is represented by the wings on the woman being born again from the cocoon into her new form or her final point in life. The hand represents the body and as you can see, it is the left hand symbolizing her divinity and creativity. Her stages of change could be recognized as childhood, puberty, and adulthood. The waxing and waning of the moon is symbolic of all changes in life including the ancient view of the Maiden, Mother, and Crone. The eye of Horus resides at the top of the circle as a bringer of change, thus enlightenment. The three circles at the base represent the two dark suns (unseen) and the one light sun that we physically see. The four trinity knots are the elements and the two are the divine union of mother and father and creativity. The two moths are the bringers of light or truth.

2. BUGS AND SYMBOLISM

The first peace, which is the most important, is that which comes
within the souls of people when they realize their relationship,
their oneness with the universe and all its powers, and when they
realize that at the center of the universe dwells the Great Spirit,
and that this center is really everywhere, it is within each of us.
—Black Elk

What do insects represent to you? An ant could signify industry
and cooperation. A butterfly might remind you that you are in a
metamorphic stage of life. A spider might represent creativity or
could even represent your web of life. The smallest organism could
hold truth and answers to some of life's biggest questions. The physical structure and social or even reclusive behavior of insects have
emblematic significance for us.

Our ancient ancestors, who could hear the life that surrounded
them on this planet, found symbolism and spiritual messages in
many forms of life. One of these ancient emblems is the Egyptian
scarab. Manley P. Hall noted that the scarab, "because of its
peculiar habits and appearance, properly symbolized the strength
of the body, the resurrection of the soul, and the Eternal and
Incomprehensible Creator in His aspect as Lord of the Sun" (*Secret
Teachings of All Ages*, 86). The scarabs were modeled after the dung
beetle, *Scarabeaus sacer*. This beetle rolls a ball of dung along the

ground with its hind legs. It does this backwards, while it faces in the opposite direction. The ancient Egyptians considered this symbolic of the sun moving across the sky, with the scarab god Khepri responsible for the sun's transit. An Egyptian allegory states that the rising of the sun is caused by the scarab unfolding its beautifully colored wings on each side of the body. The body represents the solar globe. Night comes when the scarab folds its wings back under its dark shell at sunset. Its beauteous wings concealed under its glossy shell represents the winged soul of man hidden within its earthly sheath. Because of its relationship to the sun, the scarab symbolized the divine part of man's nature; thus it was regarded as a religious symbol, a hieroglyph, and a historical commemorative.

The dung beetle doesn't cross our paths everyday, but a spider is a more regular encounter. Some of us equate the spider with its fangs and painful bite, even when we know that not all spiders are capable of biting a human. Many say it is bad luck to kill a spider. This could be because spiders catch and eat annoying insects such as flies. Others might associate spiders with wickedness because of their intimidating appearance or because of the habits of some spiders, such as the black widow, eating her mate. Yet even the black widow, after exhausting and then eating her mate, demonstrates the spiritual concept of death and rebirth.

The most fascinating aspect of a spider is its web and the spinning of the web is a beautiful act. The spider is said to be a weaver that awakens creativity and has been associated with balance of past and future, which might mean that what you do now will weave what you may encounter in the future. The web is like the universe spiraling outward or the body growing through life, and the center is the soul and heart of that life. Because of the constant weaving of new webs, spiders have been associated with lunar qualities, which relate to the waxing and waning of the moon. Just as the new moon signifies beginnings, we begin new webs of life. When the half moon is waxing, we are weaving our threads in time. As the full moon is the Mother, we are mothers in our webs of hearth and home. When the moon is waning, and our webs are worn, the dark moon Crone cuts those threads of life. All that remains are new beginnings and new webs to weave. The spider's web may serve to remind us of the beauty of our own lives and the cycles we live by. In this aspect, the spider reminds me to never let go of hope.

Contemplating the spider's web and seeing it as a microcosm of life, we are immediately drawn to how the spider's web catches food like flies. Flies are often associated with buzzing around filth, death, feces, rotten food, and so forth. Because of their annoying habit of buzzing and sometimes biting, flies have been considered tormentors. Therefore, the fly might be construed as spiritually negative. Such an association is not universal in human experience. The Chaldean god Baal was often called Baal-Zebul, which means "god of the dwelling place." The word zebub, or zabab, means "fly." Baal-Zebul became Baalzebub or Beelzebub, which loosely translated means "Jupiter's fly." Thus, at one time the fly may have been considered a form of divine power because of its ability to destroy decaying substances and consequently promote health.

The fly has not always been considered to be symbolically positive, either. The Jewish religion interprets Baalzebub as "My Lord of Flies." They changed Baalzebub into Beelzebub and turned him into their prince of devils by interpreting dæmon as "demon" (Hall, *Secret Teachings of All Ages*, 87). In Zoroastrianism, one demon is the female, Nasu. She is the demon of dead matter and is represented by the fly. Flies are found in mythology around the world and frequently represent demonic beings and are related to death. Paying attention to the nature of the fly, one might think not just of demons and death, but possibly about human behavior. Do we spend too much time over an issue that is "dead"? Or maybe a situation that needs dissolution or "decomposing"? My purpose in asking these questions is to point out that we can learn from observing the world around us, including insects such as the fly.

Among other arachnids in mythology, the scorpion has been associated with numerous beliefs. The sting of a scorpion has been an emblem of victory or protection as well as aggression. They are also associated with Venus through their ritualistic and sometimes fatal mating dance. The scorpion itself has been considered a symbol of wisdom because fire, which it controlled, was capable of illuminating as well as consuming. There is rich history about this little creature, including its astrological star formation that moves across the sky. Consider, for example, the ancient Near East tale of the Scorpius constellation. The boastful hunter, Orion, threatened to kill all of the animals of the Earth Goddess, Gaia. She sent the scorpion to kill Orion. The scorpion delivers a fatal poisonous sting to Orion's heel. Later, Ophiuchus, the Serpent Bearer, revives Orion with the antidote. This legend is eternally played out in the sky in its diurnal and annual cycles. Scorpius emerges in the eastern sky while Orion appears to die as he sets in the western horizon. Later in the annual cycle, setting in the west is Ophiuchus standing above the defeated Scorpius. Meanwhile, resurrected Orion emerges in the East. For more information on scorpion symbolism, you might want to study the *Ancient Egyptian Book of the Dead*.

Another insect with ancient symbolism is the dragonfly, estimated to have been around for over 180 million years. Dragonflies are fascinating and are certainly not considered pests, for they eat mosquitoes and other flying insects. Their incredible colors have developed through time. They inhabit two realms throughout their lifetimes. As nymphs they begin their lives in water. Through maturation and metamorphosis, they move to the realm of air. In air they can fly at speeds up to thirty miles an hour, as well as change directions instantly, move up or down, and fly backwards. Although these are phenomenal traits, they might represent lightness and instability. Yet their agility could represent mental alertness and the ability to capture or perform something in a quick and precise manner. This particular insect has not had consistent symbolism; yet I think that, like dreams, these qualities represent something different in each individual's life. It is a matter of observation and interpretation.

Like the dragonfly, the butterfly is also associated with metamorphosis. It is also associated with movement and shape shifting. Butterflies and moths go through four distinct stages of development: egg, larvae, chrysalis (cocoon), and adult. This beautiful creature can provoke the question of which stage of change or

MANNA

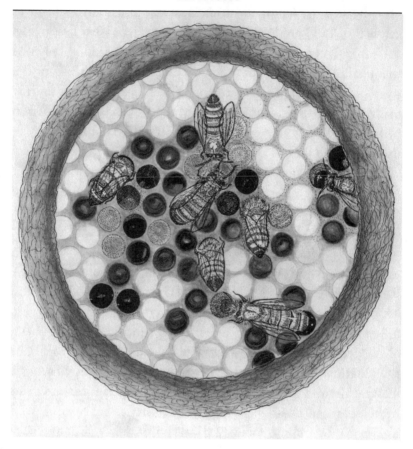

Manna is simple and I felt best represented by honeybees. It is the life essence and spiritual nourishment of divine origin. It represents pollination and fertility, which perpetuates life. This process is only enabled through the soul by tasting the nectar of life. It is the hidden wisdom. Although the honeycomb appears as circular holes, there are actually six sides, which represent the sun and its associated energies. Like the bees, we must work to partake of it. Some of the holes are black and partly filled. The ones that are light represent the fruition of our work, the divine light shining through. Manna is always there, only if we partake of it.

development in your life you are in. Butterflies are powerfully symbolic. In early Christianity they were the symbol of the soul, and in China they have been symbols of conjugal bliss and joy. Some Native American cultures have considered butterflies to be symbols of change and happiness. Another aspect of the butterfly, and one I often associate with spring, is color. Color is caused by the differing qualities of light reflected or emitted by something. What colors do you reflect or emit? What does this mean to you?

Many other small creatures have been seen as symbolic throughout time. I could never cover them all in a chapter. However, I ask you to ponder this thought: As much as we search the stars for their macrocosmic relation to us, we should search the microcosmic relationship we have with the "very small" that live inside the planet that breathes life into our existence. These insects and other creatures have as much purpose as the moon and this solar system in the cycle of life. If we keep ignoring that, we ignore the intricate balance of life in its natural, evolving state.

3. PESTICIDES

What is man without the beasts? If all the beasts were gone, men would die from great loneliness of spirit, for whatever happens to the beasts also happens to man. All things are connected. Whatever befalls the earth befalls the children of the earth.

—Chief Seattle

What do you do if you find a bug or some bugs in your house? Do you:

a) Scream?
b) Panic?
c) Call the exterminator?
d) Get out the bug spray?
e) All of the above?
f) None of the above?

The answer is (f), none of the above. First you have to realize that not all bugs were created just to bite you or make your life miserable. In fact, most of them would rather be anywhere else than in your house. You should simply remove the offending arthropod by putting a glass over it, sliding a piece of paper under it, and then carrying it outside. If this takes more courage than is available, then it is okay to kill the offending bug by hitting it with something.

Then you should find out how it got into your house in the first place, so other bugs won't follow suit. Was the door open? Did it come in under the door? Did it fly in through an open window? Was it carried in on firewood or something else? Once you have answered these questions, it is a simple matter to control the situation.

If, by chance, you are seeing a number of bugs, then basically the same principal applies except you will want to kill the bugs, as it wouldn't be practical to scoop them all up and carry them outside. Soap and water (ten parts water to one part dish soap) will kill most bugs, including ants. In the case of a lot of bugs, you should get a positive identification of the bug so you can find out about its habits in order to help you prevent future occurrences. You can generally take bugs to your local county extension service or to an entomologist at a local university or museum to get them identified.

What is it about bugs that causes repulsion in the average human being? Why do we feel a need to call an exterminator every time we see a bug? The pest control industry specializes in ridding our homes of unwanted pests. I know some of you are cracking up at that statement, but that is, at least in theory, their purpose in life. Actually his or her purpose is to make money like everyone else, and that may be where the problem lies. Many of these folks are no more qualified to be in the pest control business than I am qualified to be an astronaut or Johnna is to practice medicine. Most of the people in the pest control business are honest, hard-working folks who actually try to do a good job. However, they are limited in their success because of lack of training in entomology and because they don't understand the natural history of the pest they are trying to control; but their success is limited mostly because they don't recognize the pest at the species level.

Many of these folks, when they get a bug call, drive up to the house, park in the driveway, get out of their truck, and retrieve a one-gallon, stainless steel, pressurized sprayer (known in the industry as a B & G). Then they go to the front door, ring the bell, and introduce themselves to the customer. It doesn't matter what kind of pest problem is occurring in the house, the treatment is the same. The pest people start at the door, follow the wall to the right, and proceed to spray the baseboards with whatever pesticide is left in their sprayer. About ten minutes later, they return to the front door, give the customer a receipt, get in their truck, and drive to the next account.

This method of pest control is the one most commonly used by the pest control industry, and it is known as "spray and pray" (I coined that phrase). The pest person sprays pesticides and prays it kills something. Unfortunately it is not very discriminate in what it kills.

The industry has been trying to get away from this method (mostly unsuccessfully) and is trying to practice Integrated Pest Management (IPM). Many of the owners and managers of large companies advertise that they do IPM. The problem is that they forget to tell their service technicians. I have seen the techs from companies that advertise IPM go into homes with a B & G sprayer in their hand, return ten minutes later, and drive off. One company puts a few glue boards under the sink along with spraying the baseboards and calls it IPM. That would be like me poking you in the eye with a stick and calling it Lasik surgery.

Why don't more pest control companies practice IPM? There are several reasons. One is that it is something you have to learn, and you can't make money when you are sitting in class or studying. Another is that most people in the pest control business know very little about bugs, and you have to have a good understanding of a pest's habits in order to control it using IPM principles. If you don't know what the bug is, there is no way you can prescribe an IPM program for the customer. It is much easier to spray the baseboard and hope it works.

One reason the "spray and pray" method seems to work is because the customer had a single bug when they called the exterminator. When they sprayed the house, there were no more bugs. The problem is there probably weren't any more bugs anyway, and the pest control operator could have sprayed lemonade along the wall with the same result. (I probably shouldn't have said that—I anticipate a rush to the lemonade stand to fill up the B & Gs).

Why does it hurt to spray baseboards even if they don't have bugs as long as it makes the customer feel good? The pesticides are present on the floor and wall adjacent to the baseboard, and for a long time they are present in the air where they can be inhaled. Eventually, after breathing enough of this crap, you will start to not feel good. Since you have been having your home sprayed every month for years, you will not think about implicating the pesticides for any illnesses in your family, but they may very well be the cause.

Why else do most companies still practice the "spray and pray" method? It is easy to train technicians. There is nothing complicated about spraying baseboards. They can hire anyone off the street and train him or her to spray baseboards. If they had to train the people on the principles of IPM, on the identification and habits of common pests, and on customer education, they would never get them out on the street. When I started in the business, I had one day of training during which I rode with the service manager and watched him spray baseboards. The next day I was on my own even though I didn't know a cockroach from a caterpillar. It didn't matter whether I recognized a pest or not. In those days we used DDT, chlordane, heptachlor, phosphorous paste, arsenic, strychnine, and many other "mildly" toxic chemicals. We killed everything in a house no matter what the species or whether it was a pest or not. We were not concerned about identification of the pest as the chemicals we used were equal opportunity destroyers. If you are going to implement a good IPM program, the most important aspect of the plan is to identify the pest.

In a major case of a misidentification and almost a misapplication of pesticides, a supervisor for a very large pest control company in Florida told a perspective customer she had nematodes in her swimming pool and needed to have her whole yard sprayed with a nematicide. Fortunately she didn't sign a contract and decided to get another opinion. She called the company I worked for and I went out and found she had a swimming pool full of small millipedes. Nematodes are microscopic animals that require a microscope to see. It is apparent that the supervisor from the very large company was either incompetent or a con man. I suspect the former, but either one is a menace to society.

Misidentification is not the only area where pest control operators (PCOs) are incompetent. In another case, a PCO told his customer that the pesticide he used was so safe you could drink it! My suggestion, when the lady informed me of the pest person's comments, was to offer him a glass the next time he says something so stupid and see if he will drink it. I suppose if he did drink it, the industry wouldn't miss him and society would be better off, and it would probably qualify him for a Darwin Award.

Cam Lay from Clemson University in South Carolina and Carl Olson at the University of Arizona generously gave me the following anecdotes. The names of pest control companies have been changed to protect the incompetent.

Entomologists? (From Cam Lay)

I told you about the outfit run by not one but two "Graduate Entomologists" (they sign their correspondence that way) that treated a veterinary clinic with a power duster loaded with 10 percent AGRICULTURAL! Sevin dust, didn't I? And then wanted to argue that it was EPA's fault for changing the label.

Immovable Object (from Cam Lay)

Did I tell you the one about the Immovable Secretarial Object and the Irresistible Pesticide Man? She wouldn't get up from her desk when he arrived to spray the office. ("He wasn't very nice about it. He just said, 'Lady, you have to get up for a minute.' If he had asked me instead, I would have moved.") He sprayed anyway, around her feet. She was wearing sandals and ended up at the emergency room with welts on her toes, being one of the .002 percent of the population that's allergic to synthetic pyrethroids. We found significant residues on her shoes, on the chair, and on the re-usable nylon bag she took her lunch in every day.

How To Treat a Bathtub! (From Cam Lay)

I had a good one this week. Two PCOs, woman in a wheelchair; she has carpenter ants in her bathtub (only sees a 2–3 at a time). One PCO wants $400 to drill and treat walls in bathroom and then $60/month for a year for monthly inspections. He didn't even inspect the crawlspace or under the deck (which is conveniently attached to the house right outside this bathroom). Other PCO wanted to "help" customer save money so he told her to have a husband go buy diazinon granules and put them in the tub (yes . . . in the tub), in the crawlspace, and along the foundation, then wet them. Now . . . you must admit that he at least had read the label where it says that you need to water the granules. I've checked my labels and can't find the application rate for diazinon granules in a bathtub. If you happen to have it, let me know.

PCO #2 did check the crawlspace, but not between the insulation and the sub floor. Silly me, why would carpenter ants hide there.

Boll Weevils Eating Your Clothes? (From Carl Olson)

The boll weevil incident was a case from the "X-files" of Goofy Pest Control here in Tucson. A woman called because she had these weird worms in her house. Don't remember exact location but think it was kitchen. The PCO came out, identified them as boll weevils, said they would get in closet and eat her clothes, so she needed the whole house fumigated. The lady was skeptical so brought the bugs to me, and low and behold they were fly maggots, coming in on their march from food to pupation site. Now the question: was the PCO a crook scamming this lady or was he just so stupid and uninformed that he really believed his diagnosis? Flip a coin.

Rachel Carson, in her wonderful book *Silent Spring*, clearly demonstrated her concern for our animal friends. Her concern extended to our pets as well, particularly cats. In *The House of Life* she stated, "I have always found that a cat has a truly great capacity for friendship. He asks only that we respect his personal rights and individuality; in return he gives his devotion, understanding and companionship. Cats are extremely sensitive to the joys and sorrows of their human friends, they share our interests." What a wonderfully profound statement!

If you have pets, you should never use pesticides of any kind or use an exterminating service. Recently a lady called me and told me she hired a pest control company to eradicate some crickets from her home. Rather than use bait, which would be safe if properly applied, the PCO sprayed the baseboards. He ended up killing $2,500 worth of her son's snakes, yet didn't kill any crickets. My recommendation to her was to sue the pest control company.

In another incident reported in *Proceedings, Association of Avian Veterinarians* (1990: 112–14), an organophosphate, chlorpyrifos, was used in a home where pet birds were bred and raised for six years. The target pests were cockroaches, but after five applications, fledglings began to die off, followed by a cessation of egg production. Finally the adults deteriorated and died. The owner realized that this tragedy meant he was also in danger, and that was the basis of his lawsuit against the pest control company. The final report read: "The case was settled to cover the cost of the birds and for creating a health hazard for the occupant of the house."

Although wild birds are not considered pets, they are also very susceptible to pesticide toxicity. They have suffered massive die-off and population declines because of the indiscriminant use of pesticides and herbicides in agriculture and mosquito spraying. Fledglings are more sensitive to the pesticides than adult birds as they are often poisoned right in their nests or are fed insects that have been contaminated.

Mosquito spraying has always been detrimental to our wildlife. Not only birds, but also small animals living outdoors and beneficial insects are particularly susceptible to mosquito pesticide toxins. Massive applications of pesticides do immense damage, as there are no islands of safety where beneficial insects, small animals, and birds can hide. After applications of pesticides for mosquitoes, the target pests will be back in a few days. Beneficial insects such as honeybees may take years to recover and the effect of the pesticides on animals and birds can be debilitating. The importance of honeybees in our society cannot be overstated. Years ago China started subsidizing beekeepers and went from a starving nation to one that now feeds over a billion people and even exports food. Unfortunately extremely cheap honey from China and other countries have had a negative effect on the American beekeeping industry by reducing the number of bee-hives from six million during the second world war to just around two million today.

Pesticide misuse and parasites have devastated wild pollinators, including honeybees, requiring commercial beekeepers to manage the pollination of our fruits and vegetables. Commercial beekeep-ers are almost all migratory, moving their hives where they are most needed. A third of all beehives go to California every spring just for almond pollination, while other hives go to Washington, New York, and other apple-growing areas. One of the problems of migra-tory beekeepers is that the bees pick up and distribute mites and other diseases and spread them around as they travel throughout the country.

To help in the pollination effort, other species of bees are being enlisted to help in the pollination effort. Alfalfa leaf-cutter bees, orchard mason bees and bumblebees are all being utilized. Aerial applications of pesticides not only affect the pollinators, but also destroy many other beneficial insects such as ladybugs, assassin bugs, parasitic wasps, and other predators. Since the beneficial insects are killed, the need to re-spray the pest species is required, putting even more pesticides into the environment and making matters much worse.

In *Silent Spring*, Rachel Carson warned us about the problems widespread use of chemical pesticides would cause. As a direct result of her effort, President Richard Nixon created the Environmental Protection Agency (EPA) in 1970 and, ultimately, DDT was banned in 1972. Nevertheless, our use of pesticides is growing exponentially every year. We use more than twice as many pesticides now as we did in 1962 when *Silent Spring* was published, although the EPA finally banned another insidious pesticide, chlorpyrifos. Chlorpyrifos, commonly known as Dursban (in consumer use) and Lorsban (in agricultural use), is an organophosphate, as are diazinon and malathion. Organophosphates inhibit the normal functioning of the nervous system in living organisms, from insects to humans. The EPA determined the chemical could be harmful to children and banned the production of chlorpyrifos for over-the-counter products that are used in homes. However, there are still between eight hundred and one thousand products containing chlorpyrifos and approximately one thousand people are poisoned each year by this pesticide. The EPA ban said the chemical could be harmful to children and stops the production of chlorpyrifos for over-the-counter products that are used in homes.

The EPA, in reviewing and banning chlorpyrifos, is trying to ensure that all the older pesticides meet the tough new standards established by the 1996 Food Quality Protection Act, one of the most important pieces of legislation, in our opinion, in many years. Pesticides are used in almost all public buildings, offices, golf courses, schools, food establishments, hotels, motels, hospitals, and private homes, as well as in agriculture. Residues in our food and environment reflect many years of pesticide usage. There are continuing problems with runoff from agricultural applications, groundwater contamination, and disposal of unused pesticides as hazardous waste. Keep in mind that numerous studies indicate that pesticides may persist indoors for long periods of time. Because sunlight, rain, and microbes are unable to break down or carry away indoor pesticides, residues last much longer than they do outdoors. Some pesticides can persist indoors for months or even years after application; indoor air concentrations of several kinds of pesticides may be ten to one hundred times higher than outdoor concentrations.

A good example of pesticide misuse along with the introduction of non-native species is evident on the island of Santa Cruz off the coast of California. DDT did more than kill bugs when it was being used. It has had a major negative impact on the environment. Before DDT, bald eagles, foxes, skunks, and feral pigs inhabited Santa Cruz, all without predators. Sailors released the pigs on the island in the nineteenth century and because of their size, the foxes and skunks posed no problem for them. When bald eagles were killed off by eating fish with high DDT concentrations, a niche was opened. Golden eagles moved in from the mainland as increasing development was destroying their habitat. The golden eagles, not fish eaters, began preying on piglets and then on foxes, which are about the size of a housecat. (The skunks, being nocturnal, were safe from the eagles.) This is a perfect example of the misuse of a pesticide, DDT, in conjunction with the introduction of a non-native animal, decimating the environment in a small area and threatening the existence of a native species, the fox. In order to save the fox, the pigs will have to be trapped and removed from the island, and the fox alone will not be a sufficient food source to keep the golden eagles on the island.

In our first book, *Ask the Bugman*, Johnna eloquently stated the benefits of using hemp as a crop. We don't want to cover the same ground in this book, but we want to expand on our discussion. Comparing cotton and hemp, both very useful crops, from a pest/pesticide viewpoint leaves little doubt that hemp is a much superior product. Consider that at least nine pests (boll weevils, tobacco budworms, cotton aphids, cotton fleahoppers, cotton leafworms, cotton leaf-perforators, lygus bugs, pink bollworms, and thrips) do serious damage to cotton. Then consider that over two dozen pesticides (Acephate, Aldicarb, Azinophosmethyl, Carbaryl, Carbophenothion, Chlordimeform, Chlorpyrifos, Demeton, Dicrotophos, Dimethoate, Disulfoton, Endosulfan, EPN, Ethion, Fenvalerate, Malathion, Methamidophos, Methomyl, Methyl parathion, Monocrotophos, Oxydemetomethyl, Parathion, Permethrin, Phenamiphos, Phorate, Sulprofos, Toxaphene, and Trichlorfon) are used or have been used on cotton to control those pests. This should make anyone afraid to wear cotton shorts!

Now consider that there are only two serious pests on hemp (the European corn borer and hemp borer), and they don't even generally require any pesticides to control. Many other insects feed on hemp, but only do minimal damage and also don't require pesticides.

Having considered the two statements above, you have to wonder why hemp is not grown all over the country, as it would be a very valuable crop. Hemp belongs to the family Moraceae (mo-RAY-see-ay). It is an herbaceous annual with a woody stem and reaches a height of nineteen feet. Hemp stalks have a woody core surrounded by a bark layer containing long fibers. Hemp breeders have developed varieties with increased stem fiber content and decreased levels of delta-9-tetrahydro-cannibol (THC), the psychoactive chemical in marijuana—and there lies the problem, marijuana.

Politicians have made marijuana illegal based on private prejudices rather than good science. Alcohol and tobacco, legal substances, kill thousands of people each year, while no one has ever died from a marijuana overdose; yet it is an illegal substance. Should the use of marijuana be legalized (decriminalized), and by extension, the growing of hemp? Absolutely, there is no question about it in our minds. We support the decriminalization of marijuana only for the purpose of making growing hemp a viable industry—an industry that would provide a valuable product with the use of very few pesticides, which would certainly enhance our environment and our lives.

Pesticide Labels (This Is Boring but Necessary)

In the summer of 1990 in Carlsbad, New Mexico, a restaurant owner asked his exterminator to spray the roof of a building, ostensibly to help control the flies. This restaurant was on a main street in Carlsbad. The pest control guy dragged his hose up on the roof in the middle of the afternoon, when it was over 100 degrees, and started spraying the roof with God-only-knows what pesticide. Never mind that the pesticide was probably cooked and useless before this idiot got off the roof, but can you imagine the image he presented by standing on the roof of a fast food restaurant spraying pesticides all over the place while cars were parked below and people were walking around?

In another instance of stupid pest control, this time in Houston, a pest control operator was called out to control cockroaches in a pet shop. He sprayed along the baseboards (I have already covered how ridiculous this is) right over the aquarium pumps and managed to exterminate nearly every fish in the store. He didn't kill any bugs, but he did a good job of killing a business.

It is obvious from these true stories that many people in the pest control business absolutely depend on pesticides in order to do their job, YET don't bother to read the label of the pesticide they are spraying all over the place. Whenever you hire someone to do any pest control work for you, you should insist on getting a copy of the label(s) for every pesticide they use. You also need to read the label if you use any pesticides yourself.

The label is the information printed on or attached to the pesticide container. Labeling includes the label itself, plus any other information you receive from the manufacturer about the material you buy. "Restricted Use Pesticide" means that the pesticide has been shown to be likely to harm people or the environment if it is not used correctly. It may be purchased and used only by licensed pest control applicators and those under their direct supervision. The homeowner should not use these products. You may see a designation on a label that says "For Professional Use Only." The manufacturer and not the EPA put this on the label. I talked to an official from a large pesticide manufacturing company and an EPA officer about this wording. The consensus was that the phrase "For Professional Use Only" is put on the label to protect the pest control industry, although the "official" reason is to protect the public from hurting themselves. The EPA official said that his agency would probably not enforce that wording, as they are mainly interested in enforcing wording that they put on labels. Legally the general public can use any pesticide unless it is labeled "Restricted Use Only," although a few states have local regulations against the public using products labeled "For Professional Use Only." These states obviously think people are too stupid to understand and use certain pesticides and feel the need to protect them from themselves.

The chemical name on the label is a complex name that identifies the chemical components and structure of the pesticide. A common name is a shorter name that the EPA recognizes as a substitute for the more complex chemical name. A brand name is

the name, usually a trademark, used by a chemical company to identify a pesticide product. The common name (or chemical name, if
no common name is given) is the most accurate way to identify
a pesticide.

You will find several signal words on pesticide labels, and you
should pay attention to which one you see on the pesticide you or
your pest control operator is using. "Caution" indicates that the pesticide is slightly toxic or relatively nontoxic. "Warning" indicates
that the pesticide is moderately toxic. "Danger" indicates that the
pesticide is highly toxic. "Poison" and the skull and crossbones indicates that the pesticide is highly toxic as a poison, rather than as a
skin or eye irritant. (The skull and crossbones is probably not the
best symbol to use on pesticides as many children see that image as
a representation of "cool" pirates, enticing the child to try it. Studies
were conducted to validate this theory. Possibly a better, more sim-
plified symbol would be "Mr. Yuk," a smiley face with a "yucky"
expression—☹. This would probably have more impact on children.
Certainly adults should be able to get the same message. I wonder if
the EPA would be interested in simplifying a label in order to make
it easier for children to understand. One can only hope.) Signal
words and symbols indicate the likelihood that you will experience
acute harmful effects if you are overexposed. Signal words do not tell
you about the risks of delayed harmful effects or allergic effects.

You want to be wary of the so-called "inert" ingredients in a
pesticide also. Pesticide formulations are actually made up of
"active ingredients"—chemicals that are designed to kill the
pest—and "inert ingredients"—chemicals that make the product
more potent or easier to use. Inert ingredients often make up the
bulk of an applied pesticide. It is not uncommon, for instance, for
a pesticide to be 99 percent "inert" ingredients and 1 percent
"active" ingredient.

Inert ingredients are often toxic as well, and in a few cases more
toxic than the active ingredient. In addition, many inert ingredients may be used by themselves as pesticides; at least 382 chemicals on the EPA list of pesticide inert ingredients are currently,
or once were, registered as pesticide active ingredients. Because

manufacturers claim that the formulation of these mixtures is "confidential business information," it is difficult or impossible for the public to identify inert ingredients in pesticides used in their homes, schools, or businesses.

There are several hazard sections on the label that you should read. Look for precautionary statements about hazards to humans (and domestic animals), the environment, and physical/chemical hazards. There may be a section called "Hazards to Humans." This section will describe acute effects precautions, delay effects precautions, allergic effects precautions, and personal protective equipment requirements.

It is illegal to use a pesticide in any way not permitted by the labeling. A pesticide may be used only on the plants, animals, or sites named in the directions for use. You may not use higher dosages, higher concentrations, or more frequent applications. You must follow all directions for use, including directions concerning safety, mixing, diluting, storage, and disposal. You must wear the specified personal protective equipment even though you may be risking only your own safety by not wearing it.

Some pesticides have all the necessary instructions and directions for use on the product label. For other pesticides, more instructions and directions may be in other labeling that accompanies the product at the time of purchase. The labels of some pesticides may refer to separate documents that contain specialized instructions. Pesticide users are required by law to comply with all these types of instructions, not just with the label itself.

Pesticide use should be kept to a minimum and that is best accomplished by initiating an Integrated Pest Management program in your home or business (see the next chapter).

I would be remiss if we didn't mention Multiple Chemical Sensitivity (MCS). This is a real disease that affects a lot of people. Please don't take this subject lightly.

Laurie Tumer has MCS. We correspond frequently and I asked her to write a piece for this book about MCS because it is so important. I did have to edit it because of length, but what she has to say is very valuable and thought-provoking.

My sensitivities are greater than they were before the pesticide spraying at my home in 1998. For me, avoidance of exposures seems to be the key to staying relatively symptom free—which means I am extremely restricted in terms of where I go. I have written a letter to my neighbors asking them to inform me should they plan to spray. So far, I have been lucky, but if a neighbor in close proximity should decide to spray, I would most likely sell my home, but am really unsure where I would go.

Once in a while I forget how vigilant I must be. For example, last year when I went to a garage sale I had an unmistakable pesticide reaction. As I made a beeline to my car, I asked if pesticides had been sprayed on the premises and was told that they just sprayed their fruit trees with Sevin the day before. I also felt ill at the bank recently and found that a pest service had come the week before. Since I had a pesticide reaction to Chinese food (throat throbbing and shaking), I have called all my favorite restaurants only to find that 99 percent of them spray regularly. It has been a great shock to find out how many businesses regularly spray and how many places I have to avoid. So I don't go to restaurants anymore or most grocery stores (except for the natural food grocery stores that don't spray). I don't go to movie theaters, the bank, some galleries, most malls, some schools, and many other stores. My artwork was shown in a gallery that sprayed so I was unable to attend the reception or see the show.

I have gotten mostly used to all these restrictions. However, what really got to me recently is when I couldn't just jump on a plane and fly out to be with my family when my cousin and aunt died. I had horrible headaches when I last traveled by plane and recently found out that airplanes are also routinely sprayed. I am now sensitive to things I could never imagine like most books, newspapers, and magazines. The print burns my eyes and nose.

I teach part-time at two colleges. One school has very poor ventilation and a combination of the cleaning solutions and perfumes burn my nose and face. I often have nosebleeds and headaches and nausea. When I get home from work, I have to wash my clothes, shower, and rest. To feel so bad doing something I enjoy so profoundly is also disappointing.

When I get new clothes or even clothes that are given to me, I wash them several times to get out the smell of the chemicals. Then I place them on the line to dry and bake them in the sun. I often have to repeat the process a few times. If the smell doesn't leave within six weeks or so, I give these clothes away. I use special unscented soaps, detergents, and shampoos.

I have a hard time entertaining people at my home because of what friends sometimes launder their clothes with or because of other products they use. Because of this, when my family or out-of-town friends come to visit, they usually stay in a hotel, though that doesn't always work well either when the place they stay sprays or uses air fresheners that they then bring into my home.

In the last few years, I have found that more and more people understand MCS to some extent. They either know people who get headaches around certain detergents, etc., or are sensitive themselves to some product. That such things bother people shows in all the new unscented products on the market. However, being unscented doesn't always mean they have removed the chemicals that cause allergic reactions. When my home was sprayed with pesticides, I did not smell anything. The emotional and financial cost of this pesticide exposure has been devastating.

Mostly, I feel grateful for every day I feel well and for all the things I am able to enjoy such as gardening, taking photographs (I send most of my work out to be printed), having dogs, driving, and holding down a job, and helping others with MCS who are not so fortunate.

I am very concerned about what I have been learning about pesticides, their history, the companies that make them, and the politics surrounding them, how much is used, how they affect our environment, and the many health problems that have been linked to them, including asthma and cancer. I am no longer ashamed of my MCS (as I once was) and I have found it helpful and comforting to associate with others who have this. I communicate my concerns with city officials where I live and the college where I teach and this has caused them to explore alternatives to spraying pesticides. I am eager to see legislation passed to make it mandatory for businesses that spray to post notification. This would do much to raise public awareness and force physicians to be better trained. Until then, most people will remain unaware that their supposed flus or sudden malaise could be a pesticide reaction.

My new awareness has informed my teaching and artwork. I am working on a project called Glowing Evidence that involves the fluorescent tracer research of Dr. Richard Fenske from the University of Washington. To train pesticide applicators, Dr. Fenske places a fluorescent tracer in a mixing tank with water and after they simulate a spraying of a field or greenhouse, applicators are placed in a darkened room and what attaches to their skin and cloths glows in the dark. These haunting photographs have far reaching implications. They make visible what we don't see at the grocery store or restaurants.

I am now a member of several e-groups on organic gardening and pest control. Recently a pest control operator asked why so many people were anti-pesticide. I am of the opinion that these synthetic pesticides are at least as dangerous as nuclear waste and definitely a more insidious problem. Nuclear waste is a horrific problem but it is a problem that everyone agrees about and we legislate because of it. With pesticides there is no agreement and there is no widespread fear. The EPA tries to legislate but doesn't have the resources to test the hundreds or so pesticide products on the market.

There are thousands of applications of pesticides in any given day in the state of New Mexico where I live. In spite of this, I am encouraged that the University of New Mexico practices IPM and the City of Santa Fe has just employed a full-time IPM expert to educate the public about safer ways to take care of their pest and weed problems. Also, I'm heartened that my one voice has caused the city where I live and the college where I teach to reconsider their pesticide spraying programs. I have met many people working hard to re-educate the public, people like Richard Fagerlund, who spends many unpaid hours identifying people's bugs and recommending responsible ways to eradicate them on his website and in his columns to spare people from an experience like I've had. There is cause to hope.

4. THE PRINCIPLES OF INTEGRATED PEST MANAGEMENT

Cricket control, circa 1590

House crickets with their chirping and calling are a troublesome thing in the house for a landlord, since they often fall into the food and drink of men and animals. They can be expelled as follows: Take some carrots, cook them and add Arsenicum; spread them in the crevices, cracks and holes in which the crickets are located, and so they will die. But take good care that no one else eats any of it. In winter, a bundle of pea-straw can also be placed in the room and they will all crawl eagerly into it. Afterwards, carry it out into the cold or the snow, and they will soon grow numb and die of cold, for they cannot tolerate the cold. That is why they always remain close to the stove.

—Johann Colerus, *Household Book*, 1590

This is a good illustration of Integrated Pest Management (IPM) in use four hundred years ago. First they identified the pest and found out where it was hiding. Then they used a pest-specific bait (arsenic-laced carrots) and also a lure (pea-straw) to capture them. They got along without liquid pesticides then; maybe we can now.

Simply stated, IPM is a method of pest management that uses a variety of ways to control pests using a minimal amount of pesticides, if any at all. There are five basic principles of IPM. They are not written is stone, as different situations will require different options, but these five are applicable in most situations.

- Inspection of the premises: It is essential to inspect the property to determine how the pests are entering, where they are hiding, and what they are feeding on. All of this information is important in prescribing a good IPM program.
- Identify the pest: It is virtually impossible to control or eradicate a pest if you don't know what it is. Never guess at an identification or your control measures may not work. Can you imagine a doctor telling you that they don't know what is wrong with you, but if you take this pill three times a day, you will be fine? You wouldn't feel very confident in that medical advice, so why would you let someone treat your home

---

These blister beetles were identified as carpenter ant queens by a pest control salesman. He tried to sell the customer a carpenter ant control program.

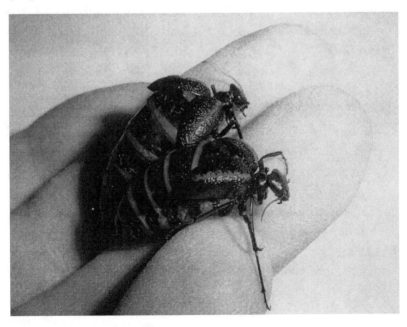

without knowing what the pest is? If you don't know what it is, take a specimen to your local cooperative extension service or a university entomologist for positive identification.

- Sanitation and maintenance: Sanitation procedures are a vital step in deterring pests, as are maintenance tasks such as fixing loose screens, repairing cracks in the foundation, using weather stripping and door sweeps, and removing ground litter near the building.

- Mechanical traps and baits: There are traps available for most pests that will enable you to monitor and control pests with a minimal use of pesticides. Baits are also available for a wide variety of pests, negating the need to spray liquid or aerosol pesticides.

- Pesticides: Liquid and aerosol pesticides should only be used as a last resort and should never be used to "prevent" infestations.

There are a number of differences between using IPM and the more typical "spray and pray" method. Here are some examples of the pros and cons of IPM and S&P as performed by professionals.

Problem—You have large, black cockroaches (waterbugs)

Spray and Pray—Spray the baseboards and around the foundation with a residual pesticide.

Drawbacks—Treatment doesn't get to the source, kills only a few roaches at a time, necessitating repeated (monthly) applications of the pesticides.

IPM—Put a capful of bleach down each drain and tell the homeowners to make sure they put the drain stoppers on all drains at night. Place Niban Bait (made from boric acid) in the cabinets near the pipes, under and behind appliances, around the hot water heater in the garage, and other places roaches may hide. Explain to customers why they may have to install door sweeps on the outside doors.

Benefits—Controls roaches at the source and bait remains efficacious for many months, negating any need for repeated pesticide applications.

Problem—Ants all over the kitchen

Spray and Pray—Spray baseboards and around foundation with a residual pesticide. Drill holes in wall and inject insecticidal dust.

Drawbacks—Usually does not control ants because the particular species is not identified as anything more than "sugar ants." Most pest control operators are very deficient at identifying ants to species, which is necessary if control is going to be successful. Monthly service usually recommended.

IPM—Ants are properly identified and a bait that is known to be effective against the species in question is used in the kitchen. Liquid pesticides are not necessary for ant control.

Benefits—Not necessary to drill holes in walls or have repeated applications of pesticides on a monthly basis. Ants are usually eliminated on the first visit.

Problem—Clothes moths? Carpet beetles?

Spray and Pray—Spray baseboards and then apply pesticides in other areas of the house without knowing for sure which pest is present. If treatment for clothes moths doesn't work, come back and spray for carpet beetles and hope it works. This is known as Trial and Error Pest Control. Monthly spraying is recommended.

Drawbacks—Too much pesticide is used when the pest hasn't even been identified.

IPM—Pest properly identified. Pheromone traps are used in the case of clothes moths. Spot treatments of pesticides are used in the case of carpet beetles.

Benefits—No unnecessary pesticides are applied and monthly applications are not necessary.

Problem—Mice

Spray and Pray—Place rodenticides all over house and outdoors. Use glue boards in house. Monthly application of spraying and baiting recommended.

Drawbacks—Mice die in inconvenient places and smell, and in some cases this can be unhealthy. Mice get stuck in glue boards and sometimes take days to die. These traps are very inhumane. Non-target animals get into rodenticides and get stuck in glue boards.

IPM—Home is inspected to find out how mice are getting in and recommendations are made to exclude them. Traps are used to control the mice inside.

Benefits—Mice can be collected, identified, and properly disposed of. Monthly application of rodenticides not necessary.

It is important that IPM procedures be implemented in all of our public buildings, in particular, our hospitals and nursing homes, but where it is most important is in our school systems. We cannot continue to spray pesticides in schools and endanger the health of our children.

Integrated Pest Management in Schools

This may be the most important section in this book. If you forget everything else in the book, please remember the information in this chapter.

In February 1995 the following story appeared in the *Albuquerque Journal*. Names of institutions and the people involved are omitted, as we have no desire to embarrass anybody.

The parents of an elementary school student are suing a New Mexico school district claiming pesticides poisoned their son. The lawsuit claims a chemical used to exterminate bugs at the school caused the boy to get ill. The suit alleges that the child was healthy prior to 1994 when he began attending kindergarten at the elementary school.

'He complained of stomach aches and headaches,' the lawsuit said. 'His bones would hurt, his eyes would be swollen and his tongue would peel and blister. He was always tired and would fall asleep as soon as he got home. He began having bloody noses, a sore throat, and lost his appetite.'

The boy was finally diagnosed as being allergic to pesticides and was told that he had a very weak immune system. The parents obtained Material Safety Data Sheets for the pesticides used by the pest control company and found that the symptoms listed on the safety sheets were very similar to their son's symptoms.

The school responded by saying they were only spraying in the cafeteria and not in classrooms. The boy's father witnessed the pest control company spraying around the outside of one of the buildings—only fifty feet from where the children catch the bus.

The suit claims the district and the pest control company continued to spray even though they knew it would be harmful and that school officials failed to look at alternative methods for fighting pests.

This is not an isolated incident. It has been repeated in public schools, universities, and public buildings around the country. The good news is that some school districts and universities are adopting IPM programs for the sake of their students, staff, and faculty. The bad news is that many more institutions are continuing the spray and pray method of pest control and people, particularly children, will be adversely affected.

According to the New Mexico Public Interest Research Group (NMPIRG) report, the National Parent Teacher Association passed a resolution calling for the reduced use of pesticides in schools and asking policy-makers to consider all possible alternatives before using any pesticides. Since then, the National Education Association and a wide array of public interest organizations across the nation have announced support for reducing pesticide use in schools.

Nevertheless, pesticides continue to be used in a number of school settings including classrooms, cafeterias, and athletic fields. The use of pesticides in our children's environment is of particular concern because children are uniquely vulnerable to toxic chemicals. According to the National Academy of Sciences, children are more susceptible to the effects of toxic chemicals than adults and may not be protected from pesticides under current regulations. Not simply "little adults," children's bodies are in the midst of highly complex and vulnerable developmental processes that regulate tissue growth and organ development. They may also receive relatively greater exposure than adults—both because of their physiology and because of childhood behaviors, which increase contact with surfaces sprayed with pesticides and other pesticide substances. Children also have a higher respiratory rate, enabling them to inhale airborne pesticides at a faster rate than adults. Very young children who put their fingers and other objects in their mouths may face even greater exposure. Also, the breathing zone for children is usually closer to the floor where pesticides are re-suspended into the air after the floor surfaces are disturbed. Finally, a building's ventilation system may also contribute to greater pesticide exposure. Some pesticides can become airborne and spread throughout heat and air conditioning systems, potentially causing a repeating source of exposure.

At a time when childhood cancer rates are increasing, and cancer is the leading cause of death by disease among non-infant children under the age of fifteen, our need to protect children's health is greater than ever. It is time we use common sense and move towards least-toxic IPM methods of managing pests.

Presently only a few states have mandated that least-toxic pest management methods be used in their schools and that notification be made whenever pesticides are applied. It is very important that every state in the country make our schools safer for our children. Not only will our children be safer, it may be less expensive than the old-fashioned spray and pray method most commonly used. According to NMPIRG, a recent survey of twenty-one Pennsylvania school districts that have adopted IPM found that alternatives are effective, less than or equal to the cost of using pesticides, and may even reduce school absenteeism. School staff reported that IPM methods deal with pest problems in a "more permanent way." Most districts in Pennsylvania were able to control pests with little or no spraying. The majority of districts reported little or no change in the cost of the pest management program; nearly a quarter reported decreased costs.

What can you do as parents, teachers, school managers, lawmakers, or students to help implement an IPM program in your area? It is time that regulators, elected officials, and school managers renew their commitment to protecting our children from the unnecessary risks of using pesticides in schools. While state officials are responsible for addressing pesticide use in schools through comprehensive, statewide policy, school managers need not wait for state leadership to implement least-toxic IPM programs. Parents and teachers also have an important role to play in reforming school pesticide use. We urge all of these folks to take the following actions:

State Policy-makers:
- Eliminate the use of pesticides in schools that cause cancer and adverse reproductive and developmental effects, and that have other known or suspected health hazard potentials.
- Develop and provide training, incentives, and materials to promote pest prevention and least-toxic IPM programs.
- Require schools to develop a program for notifying parents, teachers, and the public before and after applying pesticides.
- Ensure that school pesticide use is reported under the state's pesticide use reporting system.
- Earmark funds to implement these programs effectively.

School Managers:
- Adopt a policy that prohibits the use of pesticides in schools that cause cancer and adverse reproductive and developmental effects, and that have other known or suspected health hazard potentials.

- Develop an IPM program that prioritizes pest prevention and nontoxic methods of pest control.
- Halt routine "calendar" pesticide applications.
- Ensure only trained personnel are allowed to apply pesticides on school grounds and in school buildings.
- Keep records of all pest management activities, including pesticide use; make this information available to the public.
- Develop a program for notifying parents, teachers, and other school occupants before, during, and after applying pesticides.
- Work toward establishing a more naturalized school landscape that minimizes the need for weed control.

Parents, teachers, and students:

- Request information about pesticide use and toxicity in school.
- Monitor school pest management decision-making processes.
- Insist on receiving prior notification before pesticides are sprayed in school.
- Advocate for a district-wide or statewide pesticide use reduction program.
- Urge school managers to eliminate the use of highly toxic pesticides and adopt least-toxic IPM strategies.

Much of the preceding information was taken from a report issued by NMPIRG. The report, *Failing Grade; a Report on Pesticide Use in New Mexico Schools* (1999), was prepared by Jennifer Taylor. Johnna and I helped Jennifer with the report, as did many other people. At least twenty-six states have PIRG affiliates and Johnna and I urge you to contact your state's PIRG or the USPIRG and find out if your state's schools are implementing IPM programs or not, and to urge them to do so if they aren't. You can go to www.pirg.org to find out if your state is affiliated or not and to get more information on this very important organization.

All of the suggestions in this chapter about schools and pesticides can be extrapolated to include day-care centers, hospitals, and other public facilities, particularly where children are concentrated.

How to Pest-Proof Your Home

This may be the most useful section in the book, as it will give you information on how to pest-proof your house. Many people get upset when they see a single cricket, cockroach, or spider in their home, and they either reach for a can of bug spray or the telephone to call an exterminator. Pest-proofing your home will narrow the chances of you ever seeing a bug in your house, and the following chapters on individual bugs will help you deal with the odd intruder without using pesticides or exterminators. Follow the simple steps below and you should have no bug problems whatsoever.

- Check your outside doors. If you can see light coming in from under them or if you can slide a piece of paper under them, a bug can crawl in. You may want to install door sweeps or thresholds to prevent bugs from coming in.
- Check for openings around pipes and wires that penetrate the foundation, and seal any you find. These are excellent places for ants and wasps to enter a home.
- Make sure all of your screens are in good repair and that the doors and windows are closed whenever possible as some bugs are small enough to penetrate a mesh screen.
- Install hardware cloth on all attic, roof, and crawl space vents in order to prevent rodents and insects from entering. If you have a chimney, make sure you have a chimney cap.
- Keep firewood and other debris away from the foundation of the home, as this will attract insects and rodents. Firewood should be stored away from the house and covered with black plastic. The summer sun beating down on the plastic will discourage any bugs from setting up housekeeping in the wood.
- Go around the house periodically with a broom and knock down any spiderwebs. Spiders will not stay in an area where they are being constantly harassed.
- If you have playground equipment, make sure you plug up the ends of the pipes on the equipment to prevent wasps from setting up shop in them. This is very important in childcare facilities.

- Do not leave outside lights on any more than is necessary. Lights attract a number of bugs and all sorts of things that eat bugs.
- Cut back any branches on trees or shrubs that touch your home. Ants will often use the limbs of trees and shrubs to gain access to buildings.
- Do not let furniture such as couches, chairs, and beds touch the wall. An occasional spider or other creepy crawly that finds its way in may end up in bed with you if the bed is touching the wall.
- Cleanliness is very important as bugs like untidiness and filth. They do not do well in super-clean environments.
- Do not leave food out at night, and do not leave pet food outside at night. The latter is very important if you live in an area where coyotes are prevalent. Pet food left outside will attract coyotes, which you don't want if you have small animals.
- Inspect any wildflowers you pick for small, round beetles. These may be carpet beetles, and if you bring flowers into your home, you could inadvertently bring in these potentially destructive little insects.

If, after reading this, you still want to hire an exterminator, then there are some criteria you should follow so you can be assured you are getting the best person possible to take care of your problem. These recommendations appeared in our first book, but they are worth repeating here.

First, make sure you absolutely need an exterminator. In most cases, pest control is a luxury, sort of like a housekeeper. I hire a housekeeper to keep my home clean. I can do it myself, but I am too lazy, so I hire someone. Pest control is the same way. The average person can control their own pests if they want to, but some folks don't have the time or the inclination, so they hire someone. This is what to look for:

- Get three or more bids, no matter how big or small the job: There are several reasons besides cost for obtaining several bids. You want to make sure the company you hire is knowledgeable about your pest problem. You want a company that will use a minimal amount of pesticides, if any at all, and you want to compare guarantees. The more bids you get, the better your chances of determining competence and cost.

- Hire a company that practices Integrated Pest Management: Ask the company how they intend to treat your home. If they say they will spray the baseboards or carpet, call someone else. Except in rare cases, this procedure is totally unnecessary as discussed elsewhere in this book. Ask the company to explain the principles of IPM (as outlined elsewhere in this book). If they don't know the principles, they can't perform the service.

- Do they require a monthly contract or agreement? There is no need to sign a contract for a monthly service, as there aren't any pests so insidious that a competent pest control operator can't eradicate in one or two visits. If you want to hire someone to come to your home periodically and inspect for signs of pests or conditions conducive to pest activity, that is valid, but you can probably determine on your own whether or not you have pests. The only reason for a monthly pest control service is to provide monthly revenue to the pest control company.

- Salesmen and telemarketers: Never accept a price over the phone. Would you let your mechanic give you an estimate without raising the hood of your car? Would you expect a doctor to quote you a price for a medical procedure without conducting a physical examination to determine your problem? Why would you let anyone apply pesticides to your home without doing an initial inspection to determine what, if any, pesticides are necessary? How can you expect anyone to give you a fair price without seeing your home? Professional and competent exterminators don't need telemarketers to generate business, and they never give a price over the phone. Their good work and reputation will get them all the business they need.

- License and insurance: Ask the company for a copy of their license and an insurance certificate. There are a number of fly-by-nighters working around the country out of the trunks of their cars. All legitimate companies must be licensed by the state they operate in.

- "Safe Insecticide": Never use any company that claims to use only "safe insecticides." The term is an oxymoron. Pesticides may be applied safely, but they are not safe. The suffix "cide" means death. Insecticides, pesticides, fungicides, herbicides, etc., are all designed specifically to kill something. Any company that advertises they use safe insecticides is either misrepresenting the facts or is completely ignorant about the business they are in and should be avoided at all costs.

- Labels, Material Safety Data Sheets, Service Tickets: Ask for copies of labels and Material Safety Data Sheets (MSDS) for any pesticides a company plans to use in or around your home. If they do not have them or don't want to furnish them, call someone else. Ask to see a copy of the service ticket they will use, and ask what information will be on it. Service tickets should show the target pest, the name of the pesticide used, the EPA registration number of the pesticide, how much was applied, and where it was applied. Make sure the company plans to furnish you with all of this information.

- Ask for references: Any pest control company that is proud of its service will happily furnish you with references. Call some of the references and check with the Better Business Bureau to make sure the company doesn't have any unresolved problems you should be aware of.

QUICK PEST CONTROL CHART

American cockroaches	Niban Bait is very effective against these cockroaches
Oriental cockroaches	Niban Bait is very effective against these cockroaches, as is duct tape laid out sticky side up
German cockroaches	Avert Bait Stations and Maxforce Fast Control work well in conjunction with Victor Pheromone Traps

Household ants	Advance Dual Choice is very effective against most species of household ants. Homemade baits also work very well.
Carpenter ants	Advance Carpenter Ant Bait is effective
Spiders	Vacuuming up web-makers and using glue boards for hunting spiders will help control them.
Centipedes	The same methods used for scorpions are applicable for centipedes
Scorpions	Door sweeps on doors will deter scorpions and glue boards will help catch them.
Pantry pests	Sanitation and pheromone traps for some species will help control pantry pests
Carpet beetles	Diatomaceous earth is helpful. Carpet beetles are also attracted to soiled socks and American cheese. Cleanliness helps control these insects as they live very well in dust bunnies
Fleas	Diatomaceous earth and electric flea traps work very well on fleas
Lice	A coconut oil shampoo such as HairClean 1-2-3 is effective
Bed bugs	Diatomaceous earth can be placed in their hiding places
Mice	Curiosity traps are the best and most humane method of mouse control. The captured mice can be released
Subterranean termites	FirstLine Bait System is excellent for these termites

5. COCKROACHES

One way to control cockroaches is to catch a roach and put it in a piece of paper with a small amount of money. Give the parcel to someone who will take it, and the cockroaches will go to the house of that person.

The cockroach is always wrong when arguing with the chicken.

Cockroaches never get justice when a chicken is the judge.

—Anonymous

Cockroaches are among the most disagreeable pests we encounter. They are common almost everywhere. They migrate in buildings via elevator shafts, unscreened drains, air and heating vents, come through doors and windows, and hide in small cracks and crevices.

No diseases can directly be attributed to cockroaches. It is true that if a roach comes out of the sewer, it may have pathogens on its feet, but they are not considered vectors of any disease, unlike flies, mosquitoes, fleas, and a few other insects. In spite of the fact that they are not vectors of any disease, more money is spent in the United States to control cockroaches than any other pest. It is the number one urban pest in this country and throughout the world.

Several species are common household pests. The three most common are the American cockroach, the Oriental cockroach, and the German cockroach.

American Cockroaches—
Periplaneta (perry-PLA-neeta) *americana* (a-MER-ee-cana)
These large roaches are called palmetto bugs in Florida and Bombay canaries in England. They can grow to 1" long and are generally reddish-brown in color. The wings are fully formed in both sexes, and they are capable fliers when they want to be. These roaches can live for two or three years, although one year is normal. Palmetto bugs prefer warm, humid environments and are frequently found in restaurants, food processing plants, grocery stores, bakeries, and other places where food is present. They also live in sewers and will enter buildings by coming up the drains. They are frequently found outside during the summer.

These cockroaches can usually be controlled in a home by making sure the drains are closed at night and that door sweeps are installed on doors to prevent them from entering under a door. Niban bait is an excellent product for controlling American roaches. Residual liquid pesticides are not necessary in controlling these roaches or any of the other species.

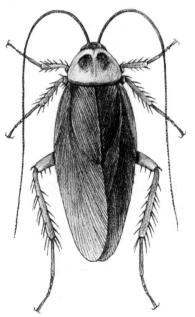

American Cockroach, a.k.a., palmetto bug. They are known to nibble on fingernails.

Oriental Cockroaches—

Blatta (BLA-ta) *orientalis* (or-ee-en-TAL-is)

Oriental cockroaches, a.k.a. waterbugs, are moderately sized, ranging from 3/4 to 1" long. They are reddish-brown to black in color. The males have wings but do not fly, and the females are wingless.

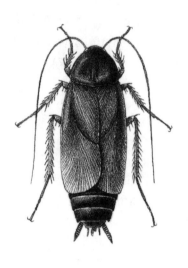

These roaches can take two years to reach maturity. The female produces an egg case that contains approximately sixteen eggs and can take forty to fifty days to hatch. This species prefers cooler temperatures than the American cockroach. It is usually found in lower levels of a building, such as basements and crawl spaces. It is also common in sewer systems and can enter buildings by coming up drains like the American cockroach. Because it prefers cooler temperatures, it is often found outdoors during cooler weather and can be found in unheated buildings.

Oriental Cockroach. This is a female. Males have wings but can't fly.

Oriental roaches can be controlled using the same methods described above for the American roaches.

German Cockroaches—

Blattella (bla-TELL-a) *germanica* (ger-MANN-ica)

German cockroaches are also known as croton bugs in some areas and Russian cockroaches in Germany. They are small roaches, ranging 3/8–5/8" long, and are a light yellowish-brown color. They have two dark stripes behind their head. These roaches are very prolific. Females produce four to eight egg cases in her life, and each case contains an average of thirty-two eggs. One female German cockroach can produce many thousands of cockroaches in a year's time if all of the roaches lived (which they don't!). Adults live an average of one hundred days. This species lives almost entirely in association with people. They are usually introduced into homes in shopping bags. If you suddenly find these roaches in your home and you shop at the same store, you may want to mention it to the store manager, as there is a good chance you brought them home from the store.

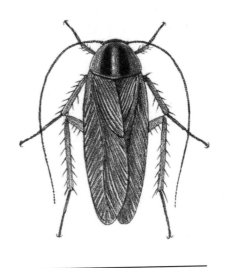

German Cockroach. One female can generate many thousands more roaches in a year.

German roaches are best controlled using specific baits (Avert and MaxForce FC are two good products) and Victor pheromone traps. Insect Growth Regulators (IGRs) are also helpful in getting these roaches under control by inhibiting reproduction. Roaches exposed to IGRs are noticeable because they have crinkled wings and cannot reproduce.

While cockroaches are quickly killed when they are found around the home or in a business, the individual roaches that become movie stars are treated well. During the filming of *Men in Black*, a representative of the American Humane Society was on the set to make sure cockroaches were not mistreated. Two hundred roaches were counted at the start of every day, and when the shooting for the day was over, they were recounted to make sure they all survived. When a roach was crushed on-screen, a plastic model filled with mustard was used so a real roach wasn't destroyed.

If you want an interesting pet, Madagascan hissing cockroaches are very popular. I am normally not in favor of people keeping exotic animals for pets, but these insects seem to do well in captivity. You can find out everything you want to know about them at your local pet shop.

Final Note—Cockroaches don't just infest our homes. Some species of ants have very small cockroaches living in their colonies and sharing their food.

6. ANTS

A drop of amber from the weeping plant,
Fell unexpected and embalmed an ant;
The little insect we so much condemn,
Is, from a worthless ant, become a gem.

A letter was posted on the Entomol-list (a list server for entomologists) recently about ant control. I would like to share a portion of it with you.

Yesterday I was gone from the office all day to teach a workshop out of town. At some point in the morning, a professional pest control person was called in to spray the break room for 'pesky' ants. He moved the microwave and dish drainer (with dishes) off the counter to the table, which is about 6 feet away, and sprayed the counter and under the sink. He also sprayed the table and behind the refrigerator. He used a tank with a hose and nozzle for the spraying.

Today there is a sign telling us not to wipe off the counter or table or to put food on either for another day. However, there has been a steady stream of people getting coffee and using mugs from the drainer, which is still sitting on the table. Of course, we are all still breathing the same old recycled air. Two colleagues had to go home early with headaches, and today several are having trouble with their allergies.

You don't have to be a rocket scientist to see what is wrong with this picture. This "professional" not only endangered the people in the office, he violated the law by not applying the pesticide in a crack and crevice method. There are no pesticide labels that allow anyone to spray pesticides on counters and tables. What makes this situation more egregious is that this individual works for one of the largest pest control companies in the country, a company whose name everyone who reads this book would recognize if we printed it.

If you have to use pesticides, and in the case of ants you don't, you should only apply them when the building is empty and according to the directions on the label. You should notify the people in the building that you will be spraying and you should check to make sure there isn't anyone with chemical sensitivities who may be adversely affected by the spraying.

A number of common ants are found in and around homes in this country. Below is a list with descriptions of the more common species. You will notice there are no ants listed as "sugar ants," "grease ants," "moisture ants," or "piss ants." These are colloquial names that are meaningless, as it is important to know what species of ant you are dealing with, and colloquial names are never found on labels of any products you may have to use.

Ants are the second most important pest in homes (next to cockroaches), but probably should be first. Ants are very successful social insects. They live in colonies where every individual has a job to do and they do it. Workers forage for food and bring it back to the colony. They can't digest solid food so they feed it to the larvae. The larvae digest the food and then regurgitate it back to worker ants, who then transfer the food to other members of the colony. This exchange of food between colony members is called trophallaxis.

There are close to six hundred species of ants in the United States, but only a small percentage of those are household pests. It is important to know which ant you have before you start a control program, as different species have different habits and food preferences. Below is a list with descriptions of the more common species.

Before you try to identify ants, you will need a strong magnifying glass or a dissecting microscope. Ants can easily be divided into three artificial groups: Ants with one node and a circle of hair at the tip of their abdomen; ants with one node without a circle of hair at the tip of their abdomen; and ants with two nodes. The nodes are the small projections on the connecting link between the second and third body segments (thorax and abdomen). The first segment is the head.

The illustrations of the ants below are taken from *House-Infesting Ants of Eastern North America*, by Marion R. Smith and published by USDA Agricultural Research Service, Technical Bulletin No. 1326.

Ants with One Node without a Circle of Hair at the Tip of the Abdomen

Argentine Ants—

Linepithema (lin-ee-PITH-ema) *humile* (u-mil-ee)

Argentine ants are small, light to dark brown, and monomorphic (all workers one size). These ants form very large colonies. It has been said that all of the argentine ants in California belong to one very large colony, although that may be a bit of a stretch. They are

---

Argentine Ant

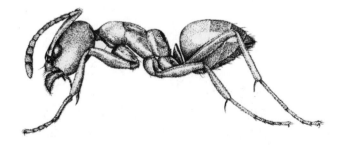

very territorial and will drive all other species of ants out of an area, including fire ants.

They will take both sweet baits and protein baits but prefer the former. They are found throughout the southeast United States and are a major pest in much of California.

Odorous House Ants—
Tapinoma (tap-a-NOM-a) *sessile* (sess-SILL-ee)
Odorous house ants are one of the most common household ants in many parts of the country. They are the ants most frequently referred to as "sugar ants." They are monomorphic (all ants the same size), dark brown, and have a very small node. These ants usually forage in single file. They are frequently found in wood ceilings where their activities cause sawdust to work loose, causing the homeowner to think he or she has termites.

These ants can be controlled with sweet baits if the infestation is caught early and they haven't become established. If the infestation is severe, pesticides (yuck!) may have to be used to eradicate them. If so, you may want to hire a professional. Odorous house ants are found throughout the United States and are often the dominant household pest in an area.

Odorous House Ant

Ghost Ants—
Tapinoma melanocephalum (mel-a-no-SEF-a-lum)
Very similar to the closely related odorous house ants, ghost ants are smaller and have a pale abdomen and legs. They are also referred to

Ghost Ant

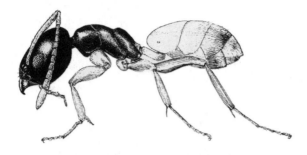

as white-footed ants. These very small ants can nest in a variety of places in a home, including inside appliances. They frequently live inside of walls and travel throughout the home on the electrical wires, emerging into a home through the electrical outlets.

The best method of controlling these ants in a home is with baits. They prefer protein baits but will also take sweet baits. Ghost ants are restricted to southern and central Florida and Hawaii.

Pyramid Ants—
Dorymyrmex (dor-ee-MIRR-mex) *insana* (in-SAN-a)
Pyramid ants make distinctive, small, round mounds in cracks of sidewalks, driveways, and sandy areas. They are one of the most common ants where they are found, but rarely enter homes. Pyramid ants

Pyramid Ant

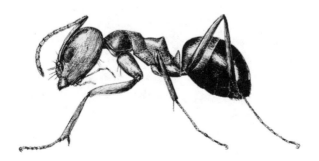

are easily recognized by the pyramid-shaped projection on their thorax that is clearly visible when viewed from the side.

If it is necessary to control these ants, the best method is to simply pour hot, soapy water into the entrance hole of their mounds. Pesticides aren't necessary for controlling pyramid ants. They shouldn't be controlled if possible, as they are excellent aerators of the soil. Pyramid ants are found throughout the United States, but are more common in the southern states.

Ants with One Node and a Circle of Hairs at the Tip of the Abdomen

Carpenter Ants—

Camponotus (campo-NO-tus) spp.

Some species of carpenter ants live inside of wood, and others, particularly in the Southwest, live under the slabs of homes and are more of a nuisance than a pest. Carpenter ants are large, polymorphic (several different sizes), and have a rounded (in profile) thorax, which separates them from the common field ants. In some parts of the country carpenter ants are referred to as bull ants. The giant ants in the movie *Them* were allegedly carpenter ants. These ants feed on the honeydew secretion of aphids and also eat living and dead insects.

Carpenter ants can usually be controlled using baits such as Advance Carpenter Ant Bait. In severe infestations, it may be best

---

Carpenter Ant

to hire a professional. Carpenter ants are found throughout the country in one form or another.

Crazy Ants—
Paratrechina (para-tre-KIN-a) *longicornis* (lon-gi-CORN-is)
Crazy ants are small, dark brown or black ants with very long legs and antennae. The first segment of the antennae (scape) is nearly twice as long as the length of the head. These ants get their name from their habit of running around erratically, rather than moving in single file or columns like most other ants.

Crazy ants can be very persistent and hard to control. It may be necessary to experiment with various homemade baits. These ants are a pest in the southeast United States along the gulf coast from Florida to Texas.

Crazy Ant

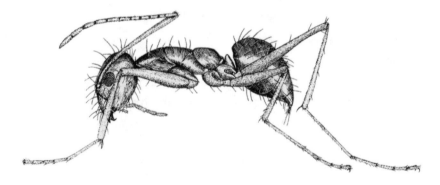

Yellow Ants—
Acanthomyops (a-can-tho-MY-ops) spp.
Yellow ants are about ¹/₈" long, light yellow in color with very small eyes, and are monomorphic. They are subterranean ants and give off a lemon-like smell when crushed. In some parts of the country they are called citronella ants. Because they are nocturnal, they are often not seen in homes until they swarm.

Yellow Ant

These ants do not take baits and require a contact insecticide. If you can find their mound, you can soak it with hot, soapy water. They are found throughout the United States but are usually household pests in northeastern and midwestern states.

Ants with Two Nodes

Little Black Ants—

Monomorium (mon-o-MORE-ee-um) *minimum* (min-a-mum)
Little black ants are very small and very numerous where they occur. They are monomorphic, and the antennal ends in a "club" that has three segments.

Little Black Ant

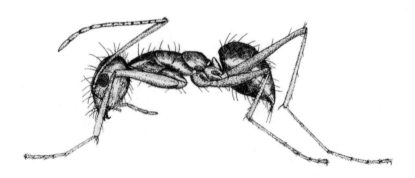

These ants are usually pretty easy to control using baits. Advance Dual Choice works very well for this species. Little black ants are found throughout the United States but are more common in the eastern half of the country.

Pharaoh Ants—
Monomorium pharaonis (fare-a-ONIS)
Although these little ants are closely related to little black ants, they are much harder to control. They are yellowish or reddish in color. They do not swarm as most ants do to reproduce their colony but use a procedure called "budding." In this method of reproduction, some workers split off from the main colony taking along some reproductives with them.

When pesticides are used, they will force pharaoh ants to bud, which actually exacerbates the problem. A comprehensive baiting program is the only sure way to treat for this species of ant. Pharaoh ants are found throughout the country but are usually restricted to major cities and large buildings in the northern part.

Pharaoh Ant

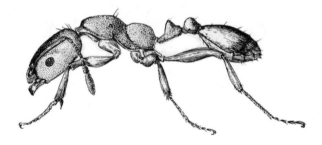

Fire Ants—
Solenopsis (Sol-en-OP-sis) spp.
Fire ants range in size from $^1/_8$–$^3/_{16}$" long. The color is variable, depending on species. All fire ants have a two-segmented club on the end of their antennae. They are dimorphic (two sizes in a colony). Fire ants have very large colonies, and when they infest

a house, they are very difficult to eradicate. They can inflict numerous painful stings when disturbed.

Several baits are labeled for the control of fire ants, but they have to be used repeatedly as the ants often will return to treated areas. The several species of fire ants are found throughout the southern portion of the United States.

Note: Only in Texas—the city of Marshall, Texas, holds a Fire Ant Festival every October. Since they haven't been able to eradicate the ants, they did the next best thing—they decided to have a festival for them. The festivities include a fire ant roundup, in which contestants dressed in protective clothing try to fill containers with live fire ants. They also have an ant-calling contest with junior and senior divisions. Since no one knows how fire ants sound, they have to be creative. Some people even dress up like fire ants. In a state that has an armadillo beauty contest and a cow-pie-throwing contest, I guess a fire ant festival isn't too strange.

Fire Ant

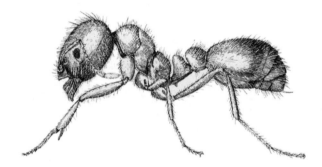

Thief Ants—

Solenopsis (Sol-en-OP-sis) *molesta* (mo-LESS-ta)

Thief ants look like fire ants but are much smaller. They often live near the colonies of other species of ants and steal the eggs and pupae from them. When another species of ant is eradicated from a home, thief ants occasionally show up looking for food since their

Thief Ant

food supply has been eliminated. They are often mistaken for "baby ants" of the original pest. Thief ants are monomorphic and have a two-segmented antennal club, which separates them from pharaoh ants, which have a three-segmented club.

These little ants will take a protein bait. Thief ants are found throughout the United States.

Acrobat Ants—

Crematogaster (Kree-mat-o-GAS-ter) spp.

Acrobat ants can be readily identified by the shape of the abdomen, which is heart-shaped when viewed from above and flattened on top when viewed from the side. They also have two distinct spines on the thorax. Acrobat ants are monomorphic and

Acrobat Ant

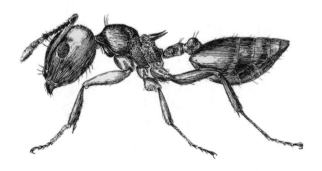

normally red and black in color, although some species are black or reddish-brown.

Acrobat ants like sweets and will often be found on plants nurturing aphids for their honeydew secretions. Controlling acrobat ants may require treating plants in the yard for aphids so as not to attract the ants. Acrobat ants are common pests throughout the United States.

Big-headed Ants—
Pheidole (fy-DOUGH-lee) spp.

Big-headed ants are dimorphic. The larger worker is known as the major and the smaller a minor. The major worker has an oversized head that is used for cracking open seeds the normal-looking minor workers collect. These ants have a three- or four-segmented antennal club that is more gradually enlarged than in other species of household ants. Most species have spines on their thorax.

Big-headed ants will usually take granular ant bait or a protein soft bait. Big-headed ants are found throughout the country and are a common pest in Hawaii.

Big-headed Ant

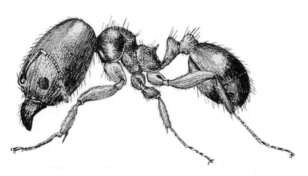

Pavement Ants—
Tetramorium (tetra-MOR-ee-um) *caespitum* (kess-PEE-tum)

Pavement ants are small, dark brown, and have two small spines on the thorax. They have a wrinkled appearance, particularly on

Pavement Ant

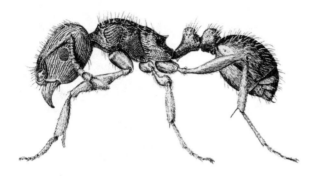

the head. They kind of look like the Dick Tracey character, Prune Face. They have very large colonies and often live under the slabs of buildings. Once in the home they will travel through walls and false ceilings throughout the structure. They can be very difficult to control.

Both sweet and protein baits are effective against these ants. They will require a lot of bait stations to gain control. They are a major pest in the Midwest and New England states but are found throughout the eastern United States. They turn up occasionally in the Southwest.

Go to the ant, you sluggard, watch her ways and get wisdom.
—Proverbs 6:6

7. FLIES

A fly persistently flying about your face indicates that a stranger either wants to meet or talk with you.

Even a lion must defend himself against the flies.

—Anonymous

No animal, with the exception of our own species, is responsible for greater loss of human life than the fly. More than 50 percent of the world's population is diseased from fly-borne pathogens and parasites. Flies cause more damage every year to crops than virtually any other insect. One particularly obnoxious fly species is known as the Congo floor maggot. The larval stage (maggot) of this species crawls around on the ground in parts of Africa looking for humans to suck blood from. Apparently beds aren't popular in some parts of Africa, and many folks sleep on the ground, providing food for the Congo floor maggot. The good news is that this fly doesn't carry any diseases, the bite is painless, and folks just ignore them.

At the same time, there are many beneficial species of flies. Many are parasitic or predatory on insect pests, while others are pollinators, and still others are important in helping break down organic material.

There are approximately 98,500 species of flies worldwide. Of that number, about 17,000 species live in the United States. Most homeowners are familiar with the larger flies found in their homes such as house flies and cluster flies. Cluster flies resemble house flies but have the distinctive habit of congregating in homes in the fall, over-wintering, and then emerging in large numbers in the spring. The flies that give people the most headaches are the small "gnat-like" flies that occur for various reasons in a home. Following are the most common small flies that can become a nuisance.

Fruit Flies—

Drosophilidae (dro-so-FIL-a-dee)

Fruit flies are small flies, about $^1/8''$ long including wings. They are light brown or tan, and they have distinctive red eyes, which make them easy to recognize. Fruit flies are also known as pomace flies and vinegar flies.

Fruit flies breed in ripened fruits and vegetables, as well as moist, decaying matter. Female fruit flies lay about five hundred eggs on top of fermenting fruit or organic material. The larvae (maggots) hatch in about thirty hours, feed for five or six days, and then pupate. The adult fly emerges several days later. As you can see, these flies are very prolific and can reach tremendous populations if left uncontrolled.

Placing a banana or other piece of fruit in a jar and putting a funnel in the opening can trap fruit flies. The flies will enter the funnel and will be unable to get out.

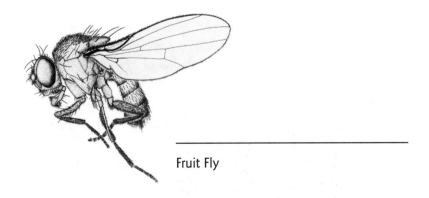

Fruit Fly

Hump-back Flies—
Phoridae (FOR-a-dee)

Hump-backed flies are about $1/8"$ long, tan or brown, and have a distinct "hump-backed" appearance that gives them their name and makes them easy to identify. Hump-backed flies breed in moist, decaying organic materials and can be a serious pest in food-handling establishments. They are also pests in hospitals and nursing homes and have been found in the open wounds of patients. They lay eggs on top of decaying organic matter, usually

Hump-back Fly

twenty at a time and about forty over a twelve-hour period. The larvae emerge in twenty-four hours and feed for eight to sixteen days before pupating. The complete life cycle of the hump-backed fly is between fourteen and thirty-seven days, depending on conditions.

These flies can be found in drains, as the larvae will feed on the gunk in the pipes. They are also common in and around trash containers. They will also breed in dirty mops, animal feces, faulty septic systems, and human cadavers, hence their other name, coffin flies.

Moth Flies—
Psychodidae **(sy-COD-a-dee)**

Moth flies or drain flies are commonly found in bathrooms. They are up to $1/8"$ long and have hairy, pointed wings, which is the key recognition feature. These flies breed in drains and overflow vents in sinks and bathtubs. The eggs hatch in about forty-eight hours and live in the gunk found inside drains. They feed for up to fifteen days before pupating. The entire life cycle ranges from eight to twenty-four days.

Moth Fly

Drains, overflow vents, sump pump rooms, and sewers are prime breeding areas for these flies. They are also occasionally found in elevator pits if conditions exist that can sustain them. You may find them in crawl spaces of houses if there are plumbing leaks.

Small Dung Flies—
Sphaeroceridae (fair-o-SIR-a-dee)
These are very small (1/8" long), dark colored flies. They are easily recognized because their hind leg in the first segment of the tarsi (the tarsi is the last segment of the leg) is greatly enlarged. You will need a good magnifying glass to see this feature.

Small dung flies usually breed in manure but can breed anywhere fruit is found. They are often found in association with hump-backed flies. A common breeding place for these flies is in moist, decaying matter, which can be trapped in cracks in kitchen equipment or under the bottom of such equipment where it meets the floor. Organic matter is forced into these areas when restaurants use hoses to clean the floor.

Small Dung Fly

Control Note

Because hump-back flies, moth flies, and small dung flies have similar breeding habits, the control methods are basically the same. Keep in mind that a great number of flies can develop in a relatively small amount of organic material, so you will have to be diligent in inspecting for their breeding sites.

- Look for organic material under kitchen appliances and equipment and in voids. Inspect any material you find for small fly larvae.
- Use a long screwdriver and scrape the film from the inside of floor and sink drains. Check for fly larvae in the material you scrape off.
- In a commercial kitchen, check inside of false ceilings and on top of coolers, ice machines, and other equipment. Look behind equipment for discarded soda cans, pieces of fruit or vegetables, and other debris where flies might breed.
- Check around trash cans or dumpsters outside, particularly if they are near a door or window.
- Occasionally drainpipes will break in crawlspaces, in walls, and under slabs. These flies can breed in the organic material that leaks out of the pipes and may enter the building through expansion joints or cracks in the slab.
- After you have found all of the breeding areas, you should remove any organic material and completely clean the area. If there are cracks in a slab letting the flies in, you should patch those cracks.
- Drains must be cleaned with a stiff brush, a cleaning agent, and some elbow grease. Drain cleaners alone will not remove all of the gunk.
- Pesticides are not necessary to control hump-backed, moth, and small dung flies.

Fungus Gnats—

Mycetophilidae and Sciaridae (my-see-to-FIL-a-dee; skee-AIR-a-dee)
A number of species in two families comprise what are known as fungus gnats. They are distinct from other flies in that one vein in

the wing is shaped like a tuning fork. Fungus gnats breed in damp soil and can often be found in house plants that have been over-watered. The maggots feed on fungi that flourish in damp soil. The best method of control is to let the plants dry out almost to the point of wilting before re-watering. This will cause the maggots to desiccate and die out. You should then put a layer of fine sand or aquarium gravel on the potting soil to deny the adult females access to the soil, which will prevent them from laying their eggs. Yellow sticky traps are also very effective in controlling fungus gnats.

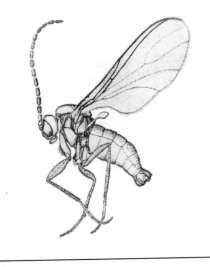

Fungus Gnat

Cheese Skippers—
Piophilidae (pie-o-FIL-a-dee)
Cheese skippers are small, dark flies with reddish-brown eyes and a bronze tint on their thorax. The body is long and thin, and it has slightly iridescent wings that fold flat over the body. This fly breeds in cheese, ham, bacon, and human cadavers. The female lays about forty eggs and the entire life cycle takes about fifteen days. Overripe and moldy cheese and cured ham products are the preferred breeding sources. Finding and eliminating the breeding source is the best method of controlling cheese skippers.

Remember that if the fly has red eyes, it is a probably a **fruit fly**. If it has a hump-backed appearance, it is a **hump-backed fly**. If it is hairy with pointed wings it is a **moth fly**. If the first segment of the hind tarsi is greatly enlarged, it is a **small dung fly**. If the fly has long,

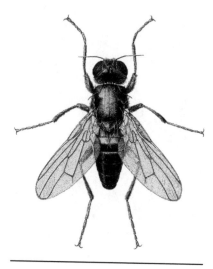

Cheese Skipper

thin legs and a "tuning-fork" appearance in the wing veins, it is a **fungus gnat**. If the fly is black, with reddish-brown eyes, a bronze tint on its thorax, and has slightly iridescent wings, it is a **cheese skipper**.

There are other small flies that will turn up in homes from time to time, but these flies are the most commonly encountered (with the exception of the cheese skipper, which is not common, but noteworthy because it infests some foods).

Final Note—Flesh fly larvae develop faster in corpse tissue containing cocaine. This fact greatly assists forensic entomologists in determining the time of death when investigating drug-related deaths.

8. SPIDERS

Many, many years ago when the earth was cold and dark, people, animals, birds, and insects could still communicate. The Cherokee needed fire to stay warm and cook with, but only a race of giants called the Fire People had fire. All the animals got together and decided that they should get some fire from the Fire People. The bear went first since he was the strongest. He came back and told the other animals that he had indeed tried his best, but he was unable to get any fire. Just then the animals heard a tiny voice. "Let me try," said the spider. They laughed and said, "You're too small."

But as each animal tried and returned with the sad news that they he or she failed, the spider's small voice was still heard saying, "Let me try." Finally she was the only one left, so they agreed to let her try. Spider fashioned a small, clay pot with a lid on it and put it on her back as she started toward the fire. She would run a little ways and stop, run a little ways and stop. As she approached the fire, it began to grow light. When she finally reached the fire, she put a small ember into the clay pot.

Immediately the Fire People missed the fire. They looked all over for the missing fire. The spider would run a little ways and stop, run a little ways and stop, until she got to the water's edge. The Fire People were almost on top of her but they were afraid of the water because they knew it would put them out. Spider slipped into the water, so the Fire People figured that the fire she had stolen had been put out. They went away thinking their fire was safe. What they didn't know was that the ember had baked the clay pot and made it waterproof. So when the Fire People left, the spider came out of the water and brought the fire to the Cherokee. This is the Sacred Fire of the Cherokee.

—Cherokee legend

Spiders are well represented in mythology, folklore, poetry, literature, and religion. In Islam, people believe that when the Prophet Muhammad first fled from Mecca, pursued by its angry residents, he hid in a cave. That night a spider spun her web across the cave's entrance so when the pursuers got to the cave, they did not search for him inside. Muslims still give spiders special respect.

Spiders belong to the class Arachnida, so named for a girl in Greek mythology. The story goes that Arachne was so confident in her weaving ability that she challenged the goddess Athena to a contest. Arachne won, so angering Athena that she (Arachne) killed herself. Athena made amends by turning Arachne's body into a spider so that she might weave the most beautiful webs with the finest silks for eternity. Hence, spiders got their name, Arachnida, in honor of this girl.

There are over 30,000 species of spiders worldwide, with about 3,000 in the United States. Two species, the black widow and the brown recluse, are dangerously venomous. All spiders are predators and feed upon living prey, usually insects and other arthropods. Some of the larger species can capture and overpower lizards, small mammals, and birds. They range in size from species only $1/20$ of an inch long to giant tarantulas that may have a leg span of ten inches.

Many species of spiders can live in the average yard, and most of them are harmless. Black widows are common in most parts of the country, and brown recluse spiders are found in many parts of the country, but particularly the Midwest. Hobo spiders in the Northwest and a few other spiders can give a nasty bite, but all in all, you have a far better chance of getting raped and murdered in this country than you do of getting bitten by a dangerous spider.

A few common precautions will eliminate almost any chance of getting bitten by a spider. If you followed the suggestions in chapter 5, you will prevent most spiders from entering your home. However, as with anything else, a determined arthropod will overcome any obstacle from time to time.

Make sure your beds are not touching the wall and that the sheets don't drag on the floor. If you live in any area where spiders and scorpions are common, you may want to place the legs of the bed in coffee cans filled with soapy water. Unfortunately, I don't follow my own advice. Recently a large, male grass spider (family Agelenidae) crawled into my bed and decided to cuddle up. I rolled over on the poor thing, and it reacted by biting me on a very sensitive part of my anatomy. The sudden, sting-like pain woke me up, and I instinctively smacked the offending spider (and my sensitive area at the same time), causing much more pain and discomfort. I spent the next couple of hours straddling a bag of ice. The pain lasted almost all day and the bite left a scar, but I survived the bite and the spider didn't. I actually felt bad about killing the spider as I encouraged it to get in my bed by having it against the wall and by letting the sheets touch the floor. If you are wondering if I have now followed my own advice and moved the bed away from the wall, the answer is no. I guess I am a glutton for punishment since a variety of life forms still have easy access to my bed.

What kind of spiders will you normally find in a home? Let's take a look at the most common species you will encounter. I am holding or letting the spiders sit on my hand in all of the pictures except the black widow. I have freely handled black widows without getting bitten, but I don't want to give anyone the idea they should handle these spiders. I did let the brown recluse sit on my finger while I photographed it, but he was in the refrigerator for a couple of hours before the picture was taken, so he was too cold to consider biting me. I let him sit on my finger so the reader could get an idea of the size of the spider. Many people think brown recluse spiders are much larger than they are. Usually when people bring "brown recluse spiders" in for identification, it is a large wolf spider or a cellar spider. Brown recluse spiders are almost non-existent where I live in New Mexico.

Black Widows—
Latrodectus (la-tro-DECK-tus) spp.

The black widow is shiny black and has a spherical abdomen. Often a red hourglass-shape marks the ventral portion of the abdomen. However, this mark may be obscure in some specimens. Black widows make ragged webs in corners, often in garages and crawl spaces. Although they have a bad reputation, it is not deserved, as they are pretty meek animals. The only way to get bitten is to disturb a web with an egg sac or to handle the spider and squeeze her. Here are several species of black widows found throughout the eastern, southern, and western United States. They can be very common in areas where they are found.

Male and female Black Widows. I brought them into the house for winter and released them outside in the spring.

Ground Spiders—

family *Gnaphosidae* (na-FO-si-dee)

Ground spiders are generally a uniform dark color, sometimes with distinct markings on the abdomen. The anterior spinnerets are cylindrical in shape and larger than the posterior spinnerets. The eight eyes are all about the same size. These are hunting spiders, and they can be collected in sticky traps strategically placed around the house in dark, quiet areas. These spiders are nocturnal hunters and hide during the day under stones, the bark of trees, and similar areas. One species, the parson spider, occasionally turns up in homes. There are approximately one hundred species of ground spiders in the United States.

Ground Spiders. Two species. The one on the right is a parson spider, which is frequently found in homes and can deliver a painful bite.

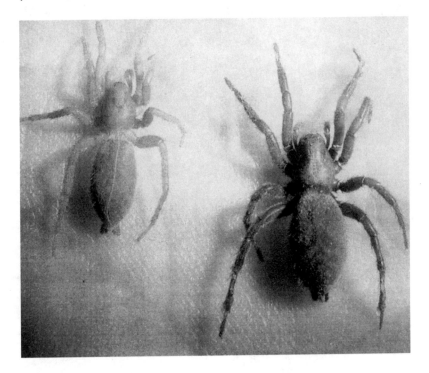

Wolf Spiders—

family *Lycosidae* (ly-CO-sa-dee)

Wolf spiders vary in size from small to very large, as is the one in the illustration. They usually have stripes on the cephalothorax. They are most easily recognized by the arrangement of their eyes. The eight eyes are arranged in three rows. The bottom row consists of four eyes the same size forming a straight line across the face. The middle row consists of two large eyes, and the third row has two small eyes. Wolf spiders are black, black and white, or colored in earth tones that blend in with the ground, stones, or dead leaves. Wolf spiders can bite if they are handled. They are hunters and occasionally turn up in homes. There are more than one hundred species in the United States.

Wolf Spider. This is one of the larger species.

Funnel-web Spiders or Grass Spiders—

family *Agelenidae* (a-gel-LEN-a-dee)

These spiders are often large and brownish in color. The eight eyes are all about the same size and arranged in two rows. The posterior

Grass Spider. A common spider found around homes.

spinnerets are long and extend out from under the abdomen where they can be seen from above. They are often confused with wolf spiders but do not have the large eyes of that spider. The hobo spider is in this family, and it has been reported to have a severe bite. Also known as funnel weavers, their webs consist of a narrow funnel that spreads out across the grass. The spider can be found at the end of the funnel. There are about three hundred species of grass spiders in the United States.

Jumping Spiders—
family *Salticidae* (sol-TIS-a-dee)

Jumping spiders are generally short, stout spiders with distinctive eyes. The eyes appear in three rows, with one pair very large, making it seem like there is only one pair. These spiders like to sit in the sun on the sides of houses or on plants where they wait for flies and other insects to pounce on. They are often very colorful. Large individuals can inflict a painful bite. These spiders may have the

Jumping Spider. This is a great fly-catcher!

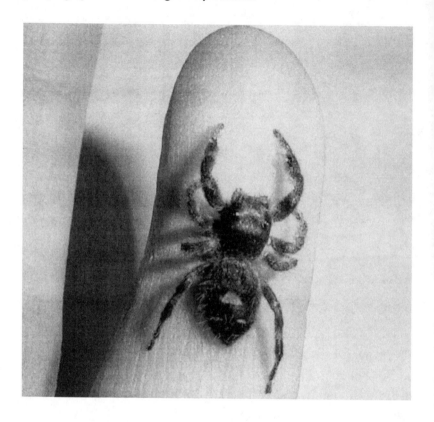

best vision of all invertebrates. Many species can recognize their prey from four to eight inches away. There are about three hundred species in the United States.

Crab Spiders—
family *Thomisidae* (tom-MISS-a-dee)

Crab spiders are easily recognizable because they hold their legs out to the sides at right angles to the body, similar to the way crabs do. They are capable of moving forward, sideways, and backward, just like crabs. The body is usually flattened. These spiders are often seen sitting on the sides of a home or in the middle of a flower waiting

Crab Spider. These small spiders are usually found sitting on flowers waiting for prey.

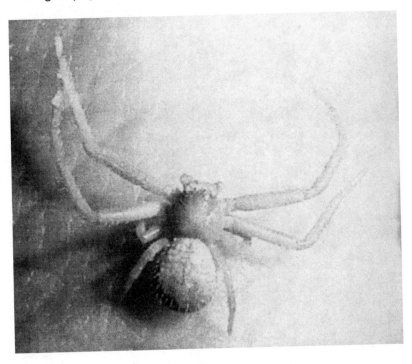

for their insect prey. Unlike some other spiders, they do not use their silk to capture prey, but in courtship, the male may loosely wrap the female in silk to restrain her while they mate. There are approximately two hundred species in the United States.

Cellar Spiders—
family *Pholcidae* (FOL-sa-dee)

Cellar spiders are light brown and have very long legs. These spiders resemble Daddy-Long-Legs, but they can easily be distinguished from them because they have two body parts, while Daddy-Long-Legs have only one body section. Some species have a marking that resembles a violin behind their heads, and they are often also mistaken for the brown recluse. They are often found in

Cellar Spider. This spider frequently makes cobwebs in our homes.

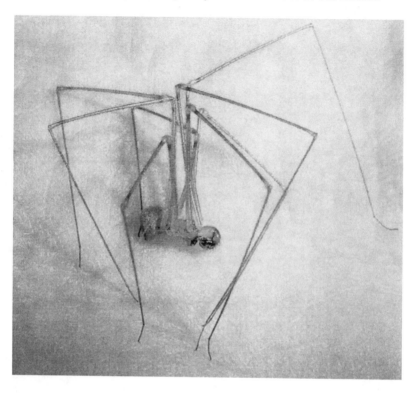

garages, sheds, crawl spaces, and in homes, where you will often see them hanging upside down in a loose web in a corner. Males and females often live together in webs. The males can be recognized by their large palps, as seen on the individual in the photograph. There are approximately twenty species of cellar spiders in the United States. These spiders are completely harmless.

Pillbug Spiders—

Dysdera crocota (dis-DER-a cro-COAT-a)
This interesting and attractive little spider is not native to the United States. It originally comes from southern Europe. It has become established throughout the United States, where its

Pillbug Spider. This spider has no common name. Please help her get a pronounceable name!

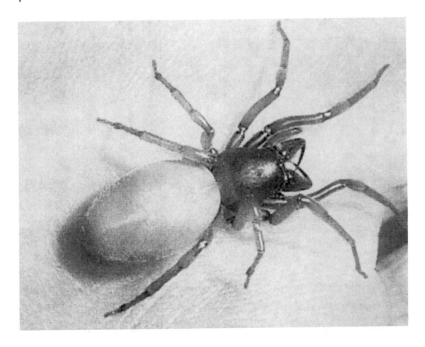

favorite foods, pillbugs and sowbugs, thrive. The pillbug spider has long fangs that enable it to penetrate the thick skin of its prey. They can deliver a painful bite if mishandled. You can find it under boards and rocks wherever pillbugs and sowbugs are found. This beautiful little spider rarely enters homes and needs no control measures.

Brown Recluse Spiders—
Loxosceles spp. (lock-SOCKS-a-lees)

The true brown recluse and several closely related species are found throughout much of the southern and southwestern United States. These spiders are light brown, about 3/8" long, and have a violin-shaped marking behind their eyes. There are related species that do not have that marking. Brown recluse spiders have only six eyes

Brown Recluse Spider. A potentially dangerous spider. This individual was in the refrigerator for a couple of hours before I photographed him so he was too cold to bite me.

while most other spiders have eight .These spiders are not aggressive and bites usually occur when the spider is trapped in clothing or bedding. Bites from this spider can become necrotic and result in tissue loss. There have been some fatalities resulting from brown recluse bites, but they are extremely rare.

Pumpkin Spiders—

Araneus spp. (a-RAIN-ee-us)

Pumpkin spiders are large orb-weavers. Although they are not normally found indoors, they are frequently brought in for identification because of their large size and intimidating appearance. They are also known as cat-faced spiders. There are several species of these interesting and attractive spiders.

If you have spiders in your home and you absolutely cannot live with them, then there are some nontoxic methods of removing them. If they are making webs in the corners or other places, the best method of dealing with them is to vacuum them up. If you see a spider crawling on the floor, place a glass over it; slide a piece of stiff paper under the glass, trapping the spider in the glass. Then invert the glass, carry the spider outside, and release it. If catching and releasing the spider takes more courage than is available, then

Pumpkin Spider. Isn't she beautiful?

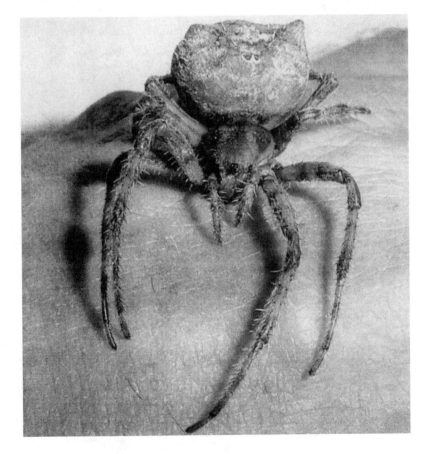

I suggest you place some glue boards in strategic places around the house. Under furniture, in corners, in closets, and other dark, quiet areas are good places. Make sure they are not where kids or pets can interact with them. The spiders will get caught in the glue boards when they are prowling around the house looking for bugs to eat. Pesticides are never necessary for spider control. In fact, they may do you and your family more harm than any of the spiders.

Spiders have been demonized in the media, in Hollywood, in urban legends, and by people who have a vested interest in selling pesticides. I can think of no animal less deserving of all the vile rhetoric attached to these little creatures. Spiders are our friends!

A NOISELESS, patient spider,
I mark'd, where, on a little promontory, it stood, isolated:
Mark'd how, to explore the vacant, vast surrounding,
It launch'd forth filament, filament, filament, out of itself;
Ever unreeling them—ever tirelessly speeding them.

And you, O my Soul, where you stand,
Surrounded, surrounded, in measureless oceans of space,
Ceaselessly musing, venturing, throwing—seeking the spheres,
*   to connect them;*

Till the bridge you will need, be form'd—till the ductile anchor
*   hold;*
Till the gossamer thread you fling, catch somewhere,
*   O my Soul*

        —Walt Whitman, *Leaves of Grass* (1900)

9. CENTIPEDES AND SCORPIONS

If you see one of those thousand-legger bugs crawling and you can kill it with the palm of your hand, it will bring you excellent luck.
—Anonymous

Several kinds of centipedes can be found throughout the United States. The one in the illustration above is most commonly found in the Southwest. The other common centipede, known as the house

---

Desert Centipede. This large species can deliver a very painful bite.

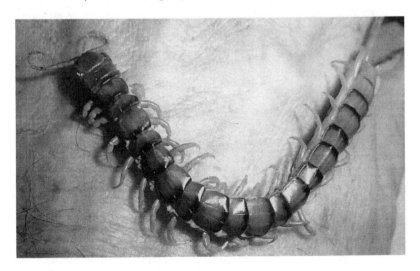

centipede, is found throughout the United States. This centipede has much longer legs than its southwestern cousin and only gets to be about an inch long, while the one in the illustration may reach five inches.

Centipedes are rather unpleasant-looking creatures and will generate a call to a pest control company faster than any other bug. Most are short-tempered and will bite at the slightest provocation. It is very difficult to handle a centipede without getting bitten. The venom is particularly unpleasant, and the bite can be very painful in some individuals, while other folks hardly notice a bite (I am in the latter category). Several years ago I was dreaming something was biting my shoulder and when I woke up, I found a centipede attached to my shoulder with its fangs. I brushed it off, jumped out of bed, and started smacking it with my hand. Unfortunately, the bed kept giving way so I wasn't accomplishing anything except making it mad. If I could have reached my gun on the dresser, I believe I would have shot it. Meanwhile, my cat was lying on the floor watching me pound the bed and act like an idiot. Finally, I brushed the centipede to the floor and hit it with a shoe. Once again, the next morning I felt bad about killing it, but at 2:00 a.m. I am not a very rational person.

The house centipede is common in basements and crawl spaces throughout its range. The larger desert centipede from the Southwest is generally only rarely found in homes, but because of its size and appearance, it is usually noticeable. The best method of controlling centipedes is to prevent them from coming in the house. Door sweeps are effective in preventing centipedes, as are screens on any crawl space vents.

If they are already in the home, glue boards are effective in catching centipedes. Pesticides are not necessary for controlling centipedes in the home.

Scorpions are nocturnal predators and are found from the southeastern United States west to California and north to Oregon. They have a stinger on the "tail" that can inflict a painful sting if they are handled or trapped. Only one species, the bark scorpion found in extreme southwest New Mexico and Arizona,

Emperor Scorpion. This is a popular "pet" species. It is found in Africa.

has been responsible for fatal stings. Scorpions spend the day hiding under ground debris or in burrows. When they emerge at night, they can often be found with an ultraviolet light, as scorpions glow under the light.

Large, black emperor scorpions are often sold in pet shops and are popular with exotic pet enthusiasts. These scorpions are not particularly dangerous, but I do not believe they should be sold in stores. I found a very dangerous scorpion in a pet shop a few years ago, and the owner had no idea what species it was or how dangerous it was. Some animals are fine as pets, but spiders, scorpions, and centipedes are not in that group in my opinion.

Scorpions and centipedes can be kept out of your home by following the recommendations in the "How to Pest Proof your Home" section of the book. Pesticides are never necessary to control these interesting animals.

Final Note—There is one species of centipede, the giant desert centipede, in the Southwest that is capable of killing and eating mice.

10. STORED-PRODUCT PESTS

Stored-product pests (SPPs) cause loss in three different ways: they destroy large quantities of food and other products; they contaminate and spoil far more food than they eat; and they can cause disease in people and domestic animals.

One human disease caused by SPPs is intestinal acariasis, which is an infestation of the intestine by cheese mites, sugar mites, or grain mites. Bites from predaceous stored-food mites also cause copra itch, grocher's itch, and grain itch, a symptom of all of which is severe dermatitits.

Insects that infest whole grain such as corn, rice, barley, and wheat include rice weevils, granary weevils, cadelles, lesser grain borers, and anguoumois grain moths. Insects infesting broken grains, flour, beans, peas, dried fruits, nuts, and chocolates include confused flour beetles, red flour beetles, flat grain beetles, spider beetles, bean weevils, Mediterranean flour moths, and Indian meal moths. Insects that feed on meats and cheeses include larder beetles, hide beetles, and red-legged ham beetles. Insects that are general feeders on stored foods include saw-toothed grain beetles, merchant beetles, drugstore beetles, and cigarette beetles. Various species of mites may infest flour, cheese, dried fruits, dried meats, grains, sugar, and other products. Some species are predaceous on the larvae of SPP beetles, but will attack and bite people.

Indian Meal Moth—

Plodia (PLO-dee-a) *interpunctella* (inter-PUNK-tella)

These little pests are generally brought into a home in groceries. They are often found in sealed food products and some species are capable of boring out of sealed boxes, crawling along a shelf, and infesting other foods. Although there are a number of different types of SPPs, the methods for controlling them are basically the same.

- All food products should be removed from all kitchen cabinets, particularly those that contain susceptible food products that may be infested.
- The cabinets should be cleaned very thoroughly with a disinfec-tant, with extra care that the space between the shelves and the cabinet walls not be over-looked. SPPs can live in loose food scraps that get wedged in these areas.
- The food products should be thoroughly inspected for insects. Examine each box for pinhead size holes. Any infested food should be discarded.
- Only foods that are sure to be free of pests should be placed back in the cabinet. If in doubt, throw it away.
- Notify the manager of the store where you shop so she/he is aware of the problem.

Indian Meal Moth.
Very common in homes.

- Spraying pesticides in kitchen cabinets is not a good idea for obvious reasons. Sanitation is very important in preventing these pests from becoming established.

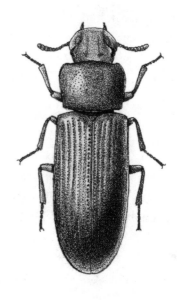

The beetle shown above is one of many species that infests our food products. The good news is that the treatment for most of the species is the same, so you don't have to try to identify each species.

Final Note—Back in classical times, one method of keeping bugs out of a storage bin full of food was to tie a toad by the leg to the door.

Confused Flour Beetle. Very common stored-product pest.

11. FABRIC PESTS

Fabric pests and stored-product pests are often the most mis-identified pests when homeowners call a pest control company. One lady called and told me that her exterminator told her she had codling moths in the closet. Since codling moths only eat apples, I asked her if she had an apple tree in the closet. If she didn't, then the fellow made an erroneous identification.

The two most common fabric pests you will encounter are carpet beetles and clothes moths. There are several species in each group, but the specific identification isn't important in this chapter.

Carpet beetle larvae feed on a wide variety of foods, including wool and cotton fabrics. Other foods include hair, leather, bird's nests, and the foods that we eat. The adults do not do any damage as they feed on the pollen of flowers. Carpet beetles are often

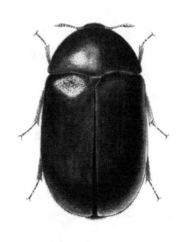

Carpet Beetle.

introduced into a home on cut wildflowers. It is important to carefully inspect any flowers you pick for carpet beetles. Adult carpet beetles resemble small ladybugs and are black or brown mottled with white or yellow. Larvae are brown, hairy, and tapered or carrot-shaped. Carpet beetles have what is known as a complete metamorphosis, meaning they lay eggs, which develop into the damaging larvae. After feeding for a while, the larvae go into a pupal state and finally emerge as an adult beetle.

Clothes moths are small, golden or buff-colored moths with a tuft of reddish hairs on their heads. Larvae are about ??" long and creamy white in color. Clothes moths are sometimes confused with another common household pest, the Indian meal moth. The latter moth has bi-colored wings, half gray and half copper, which make them distinctive; plus, they do not have the tuft of hairs on the head.

As with the carpet beetles, the larval stage of the clothes moth does the damage. The adult female has a life cycle of about two weeks, during which time she doesn't feed. She will lay her eggs on woolen or cotton products and other edible products. The larval stage feeds for about a month before pupating, but can stay in the larval stage for up to two and a half years.

Control of Fabric Pests

Controlling these pests does not require any pesticides, but does require time and effort on your part.

- Prevention is the best method of control. Carpet beetles are particularly fond of soiled clothes, so all clothes should be cleaned before being stored.
- Always check cut flowers for adult carpet beetles before bringing them in the house.
- Set out pheromone traps for clothes moths. They will capture males, stop the breeding process, and let you know they are present.
- If you find adults of either bug, carefully inspect all woolen and cotton materials for signs of the larvae.

- If you find any larvae, have the material dry-cleaned or brush with a stiff brush. Dry cleaning is preferred.
- Vacuum frequently and thoroughly. Carpet beetles can do quite well living on dust bunnies.
- If you have to use an insecticide, treat the area where the larvae are with a pyrethrin-based pesticide. Repeat as necessary in a week or so.
- It is not necessary to call a pest control company if you catch these pests early.

Many times I have seen carpets stained from pesticides sprayed along the wall by someone trying to control carpet beetles by spraying the baseboards. Actually I have seen more carpets ruined by the pest control industry than I have by carpet beetles.

If you want to make some neat homemade traps for these insects, all you need is American cheese, tuna fish oil, and flypaper. Place some American cheese on some soiled socks in a corner of a room and any carpet beetle larvae will flock to it. You can then destroy them while they are gathered around the socks and cheese.

For clothes moths, dip a cotton ball in some tuna fish oil and then stick the dry side to some flypaper. The tuna fish will attract the moths, which will get stuck on the flypaper.

Final Note—While fabric pests can be very destructive to clothing, another insect, the silkworm, is a major producer of silk. Silk is cultivated in Japan, China, France, Italy, and Spain, although artificial fibers are replacing silk in much of the textile industry. The silk industry still generates $200–$500 million annually, however.

12. FLEAS

The arithmetic flea
adds to your misery,
subtracts from your pleasure,
divides your attention,
multiplies like the devil.

—Anonymous

Fleas are interesting insects with a prominent place in history. The adults of some species transmit the plague bacillus (*Yersinia pestis*), which was responsible for the deaths of millions of people. Plague, along with famine and desertions, killed 95 percent of the Christian army in 1190 during the Crusades and had a major impact on Xerces' invasion of Greece when he entered Thessalonia with 800,000 men and lost 300,000 of them. In 1347, the first cases of the plague known as the Black Death appeared in Europe, and the disease was well established by 1348. The plague was so infectious that whole towns ceased to exist and fleeing people spread the disease far and wide. Before the end of the outbreak, about a third of the population of Europe was dead; this is the highest percentage of a population ever killed by an epidemic. The Black Death was so devastating that there were not enough people left in some areas to bury the dead. In 1664 and 1665, the plague returned to London, killing 100,000 people. It struck again in Yunnan, China, in 1892, spread throughout south Asia, and ended up killing six million people in India. It reached Hawaii and South America in 1899, and San Francisco had an outbreak in 1904 that left 122 dead.

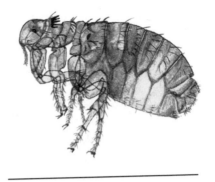

A bacillus spread by the Oriental rat flea, which parasitized commensal rodents such as Norway rats, caused the plague that started in Europe and Asia. When the plague reached California by way of rat-infested ships, the

This is a copy of the original drawing of a flea by Johnna, which is featured in our first book, *Ask the Bugman.*

local rodent fleas became a vector of the disease, and now many species are potential vectors of the plague. For instance, in New Mexico alone, there are 107 species of fleas, and almost a third of them are possible vectors of the plague.

There are four basic types of plague associated with fleas.

- **Bubonic Plague**—In Bubonic plague, the blood is infected and the bacilli are arrested in the lymph glands, particularly those in the groin and under the armpits, resulting in inflamed glands, which suppurate. The mortality rate for Bubonic plague ranges from 40 to 70 percent.
- **Septicemic Plague**—In most serious cases, the lymph glands fail to arrest the bacilli, which appear in large numbers in the blood. Numerous hemorrhages occur under the skin and turn black, accounting for the name "Black Death." This form of plague is very virulent and death nearly always occurs.
- **Pneumonic Plague**—In this condition, when the bacilli are in the lungs, we have the most dangerous form of plague from a public health standpoint, since it is spread rapidly through contact and coughing, as well as by the consumption of contaminated food. This form of plague nearly always results in

mortality of over 90 percent. It is now thought that the initial fourteenth-century outbreak was this form since the spread was so rapid.

- **Sylvatic Plague**—In this form, the virulence is greatly diminished. Sylvatic plague is apparently not highly contagious to man, as there are very few human deaths each year. Sylvatic plague is spread by the fleas on wild rodents, rather than the commensal mice and rats responsible for the other types of plague. There are normally ten times as many cases of this type of plague in cats as there are in humans.

Symptoms of plague include fever, chills, body aches, sore throat, headache, and weakness. These may be followed by abdominal pain, nausea, vomiting (bloody at times), constipation, or diarrhea and black and tarry stools. A cough may develop and may be accompanied by sputum. Shortness of breath and a stiff neck are also symptoms.

Plague is easy to avoid if a few common sense precautions are taken. Never skin a dead animal without wearing gloves and a long-sleeved shirt. Never camp near rodent burrows. Keep non-toxic flea collars on your pets, particularly cats, if you live in a neighborhood with a lot of ground squirrels or prairie dogs. Never touch or approach an animal that appears injured or lethargic.

Fleas that have the plague are particularly dangerous. When a flea ingests plague bacilli from a reservoir (a ground squirrel, for example), the bacilli coagulate in the flea's gut, preventing it from getting enough nourishment to sustain it. Consequently, the flea is always hungry and will bite repeatedly. When the flea ingests blood from a human or cat, it cannot swallow the blood, so it regurgitates it with some of the plague bacilli into the bite site of the victim, thus causing the plague.

Various methods of flea control have been tried over the ages, some effective, some silly. In Europe during the middle ages, women wore a flea trap around their necks to collect fleas. It consisted of a sticky tube inside a perforated tube that hung by a ribbon around the neck. Seeking shade, fleas entered the tube's holes and were caught on the sticky trap inside. To alleviate the effects of the fleabites, women kept long, ivory sticks to push through their elaborate coiffures and scratch their scalps. It is thought women began shaving their legs and armpits, not for aesthetic purposes, but to discourage fleas and lice.

Men, of course, weren't immune to flea and louse attacks, but they didn't seem to mind them. St. Francis of Assisi not only tolerated them, he embraced bodily parasites. To him they were the "pearls of poverty." Cardinal Bellamine, bastion of the Counter Reformation who was canonized in 1930, said about fleas, "We shall have Heaven to reward us for our suffering, but these poor creatures have nothing but the enjoyment of this present life."

In Africa and tropical climates, cow dung spread over the floor and hardened (often patterned with motifs) is said to keep fleas away. Hungarian shepherds were known to grease their linens with hog lard, rendering themselves disgusting even to fleas. In Greece, fires were kindled on St. John's Eve (June 23) and local youths jumped over them. This resulted in a general purgation of not only fleas, but sins also.

If you have an infestation of fleas in your home and you do not want to call an exterminator, you can control them yourself if you are careful. First, you should steam clean all of your upholstered furniture to kill any fleas or flea larvae or eggs present. Next, brush some diatomaceous earth (DE) into your carpet and leave it for five days before vacuuming it up. Be sure to wear a dust mask when using DE as it may irritate your nose and throat. After vacuuming up the DE you should be relatively flea free. You may have to repeat the process if a few fleas survive the treatment. Electric flea traps are also relatively successful in capturing fleas, although they probably won't eradicate a flea problem on their own.

If you have pets, you should take them to the vet and get them treated at the same time you are treating your house. If you have a large infestation in your yard, you will probably have to hire someone to spray the yard. There are no good foolproof methods of treating a yard for fleas without using some pesticides. Make sure you get a copy of the label and Material Safety Data Sheet for any product used in your yard.

Several years ago a pest control operator was called to a home in east Texas. He found some small, jumping insects in the kitchen and bathroom and immediately identified them as fleas. He proceeded to do a flea job on the house, which entailed spraying the carpet and furniture in the living room (although the bugs were in the kitchen and bathroom). He then collected his money and left. A week later the lady of the house called him and said the "fleas" were still there. He returned and repeated the process. After another week, the lady called another pest control company out to get a second opinion. The second fellow correctly identified the insects as common springtails, which do not bite and cause no damage. He also correctly told the lady how she could control them herself with soap and water. Fortunately, for the sake of humanity, her husband was a lawyer and he sued the first company for malpractice, forcing it out of business. I am generally not a big fan of litigation, but in this case it was important to put the first pest control operator out of business before he killed someone because of his incompetence.

Final Note—A flea can jump a distance of 150 times its own body length, which would be the equivalent of a human doing a standing broad jump of a quarter mile.

13. LICE

Diodorus (30 BC) stated that lice originated from human skin and perspiration so there was no reason to kill them.

Louse Inspection in Houston

I remember getting a call to go to a house in Houston in 1975. When I got to the house, the lady of the house let me in and told me she was being bitten by something and wanted me to determine what it was and to get rid of it. I should have suspected this would be a strange case because her husband was sitting on the couch smoking a joint, and he was stoned to the max.

The young lady asked me to look through her hair for lice. Feeling very nervous, I ran my fingers through her hair with one hand while shining a flashlight on her head with the other.

Crab Louse.

This was a bit nerve-racking, especially since I couldn't find anything. She then stepped back, dropped her shorts (no underwear), and asked me to examine her genital area for bugs, as she was also itching in that area. Feeling very foolish, I dropped to my knees and focused my flashlight on her vagina, trying to figure out how to move the hair aside without actually touching her. Finally I pulled a pen out of my pocket and started searching through her pubic hair. After what seemed like two hours, but was probably only two minutes, I stood up and said I didn't see anything. I was more than embarrassed, and in order to make my embarrassment less noticeable, I quickly turned my back to her and started talking to her husband, who was laughing himself silly, probably because of my obvious embarrassment. I recommended that they go to the pharmacy and get some A-200 Pyrinate, which was the only thing I knew of at the time, and then I left there as quickly as I could. I am not a prude by any stretch of the imagination, but I was totally unprepared for that service call and didn't know how to react.

During the middle ages, lice were thought to be a sign of holiness by the monks. The more lice a monk had, the holier he was. Body lice, however, were a major cause of typhus (head lice and pubic lice do not carry the disease), and epidemics altered the course of history. Napoleon entered Russia with about 450,000 men and lost about 80,000 of them to typhus and dysentery. When he finally retreated from Moscow in 1812, only 6,000 men made it back.

How to Control Lice

The head louse is specific to the head area and is a different type than the body louse, which is found on other hairy parts of the body, and the pubic louse (crab louse), which is found in the pubic area. Lice do not jump but move from person to person by swinging off hairs like monkeys in trees. Most transmission occurs by hair touching hair. Occasionally body lice can be transferred from one person to another by lice that are hiding in clothing, hats, and furniture. Head lice and pubic lice attach their eggs to hairs of the host, while body lice may lay their eggs in clothing or on furniture.

Combing the hair nightly with coconut oil can control lice. Infestations can be eliminated in as little as three days using this method. You should use a nit comb for this, and the best ones are manufactured in India, Pakistan, the Middle East, and South East Asia. Commercial nit combs made in the United States seem to be inferior for removing nits.

Many lice have developed a resistance to over-the-counter pesticide shampoos. Besides, why would you want to use a pesticide on your head when coconut oil will serve the purpose just as well, if not better? If you can't find a coconut oil shampoo, there is a product called HairClean 1-2-3, which is made from coconut oil, ylang-ylang, and anise oils. It is manufactured by Quantum (1-800-448-1448 or www.hairclean.com).

Final Note—"To rid yourself of lice, take one of them into the graveyard and shoot it; the rest will leave" (Anonymous).

14. BED BUGS

The June bug hath a gaudy wing,
The lightning bug a flame,
The bed bug hath no wings at all,
But he gets there just the same.

—Anonymous

Bed bugs, like lice, have been the constant companion of man for centuries. The earliest writings on natural history mention them. They have a variety of names, including chinches, mahogany flats, wall lice, and redcoats. These interesting little insects are about a fifth of an inch long and oval in shape.

Bed bugs are active at night, crawling out of their hiding places and often traveling considerable distances in order to find a meal. They hide during the day in a variety of places including mattresses and box springs; in the slots where headboard and footboard slats are inserted; behind pictures and posters on the wall; in other furniture such as nightstands; behind baseboards; under carpets; and in boxes. Bed bugs are gregarious and large numbers of them may hide in a convenient place.

These creatures of the boudoir, not surprisingly, have developed an incredible sexual deviation. The male bug possesses a stout, scimitar-like penis with which he stabs and punctures the female abdomen at a point far from her vagina. Having assailed the female, the male injects copious amounts of semen into her abdomen. It has been suggested that there are some components of the semen that may actually nourish the female in lieu of a blood meal. Some sperm do, however, swim through her abdominal cavity and eventually arrive at her reproductive organs, where they accumulate in sacs called sperm reservoirs, eventually fertilizing her eggs. Eggs are deposited in hiding places, often along the seams of a mattress. The young hatch in about ten days. The complete life cycle from egg to adult requires between thirty-seven and 128 days, depending on conditions. Nymphs can survive prolonged starvation so the life cycle may be extended considerably.

People differ in their sensitivity to bed bug bites. In some people, such as myself, the bite produces no reaction, but in others, swelling and irritation in response to certain proteins in bed bug saliva may occur. There is no evidence that bed bugs are vectors

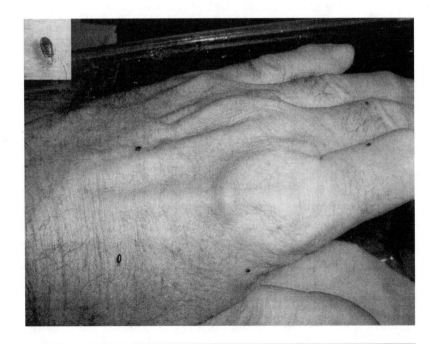

Bed Bug nymphs feeding on my hand. Close-up of a bug in upper left-hand corner.

of any disease. The bites should be washed with soap and water, but if itching is severe, some relief may be achieved by dabbing the bites with calamine lotion.

I have been feeding a "colony" of bed bugs I use in seminars for some time by periodically sticking my hand in their cage. Their cage consists simply of a one-gallon plastic terrarium with some tissue paper in it. The bed bugs hide in the folds of the tissue and crawl up on my hand and feed when I place it in their cage (see figure at beginning of this chapter). It takes adults about five minutes to obtain a full meal while the smaller nymphs require less time. Once they are full of blood, they scamper off my hand and drop back into the tissue paper to hide and, eventually, molt.

How to Control Bed Bugs

One sign that you may have bed bugs even if you don't develop any symptoms from their bites is the presence of blood spots on the sheets. This is actually fecal matter as bed bugs normally poop right after feeding. Bites on the body from bed bugs will usually be on the trunk (or abdomen) rather than on the extremities. The bite marks are often found around the waist on the underwear line. If you sleep nude, the bites may be anywhere on the abdomen and sometimes the legs.

When controlling bed bugs, the most important part of the procedure is inspecting the room and finding all of their hiding places. If the infestation is relatively new, you should be able to control them without using an exterminator. If they are severe, you may want to hire a professional. See chapter 20 for hints on hiring a pest control operator.

First, you should completely take apart the bed. Place the mattress and box spring upright against a wall and remove the slats from the footboard and headboard. Put all of the linen in a washing machine or a plastic bag. Now inspect along the seams of the mattress and box spring. Then inspect around any buttons on those pieces. If there are any tears in either item, try to inspect inside the rip. Now lightly dust some diatomaceous earth along each seam, around each button, and inside any rips in the fabric. You can use a bellows duster for this (Crusader is one brand). Repair any tears in the fabric of the mattress or box spring. Now inspect the wood framing of the bed, making sure to look inside the slots where the slats fit. Dust this area with diatomaceous earth also.

Look behind any pictures or posters on the wall, in and under any boxes on the floor in the room, behind the baseboard if present, and under the edges of carpet. Check in and around any dressers or nightstands in the room. Dust any voids or hiding places where bed bugs may hide. Any individual bugs you find during the inspection can be sprayed with a mixture of soap and water (one part soap to ten parts water). This mixture will kill bed bugs and most other soft-bodied insects.

Residual pesticides are rarely necessary for bed bug control, unless the infestation is very heavy. Diatomaceous earth works very well if applied as outlined above. Keep in mind, this is a slow, painstaking process, but you can save yourself a lot of money by doing this yourself.

Final Note—"Bug" is a Celtic word for ghost or goblin, probably because the Celts considered bed bugs terrors of the night.

15. MICE

In 1970 we got a call for mice in a meat market in a slummy area of Miami. When we got there, during business hours, we could see mice running all over the place under the floor slats. We asked the manager what he wanted us to do and he said to do something right now. We proceeded to dust under the slats with DDT. The DDT dust was filling the store, settling on the meat, people, and everything else. No one complained! The guy called a couple of days later and said the mice were dead. (He didn't say how his customers fared.) If we did something like that in this day and age, we would be in jail for the rest our lives, and rightfully so.

Mice often occur in very large numbers. Australia, in particular, has enormous population explosions occasionally. The following excerpts from Australian newspapers will help illustrate the scope of the problem in bad "mouse" years:

'I've gone into the kids' room at night and seen mice eating at the corners of their mouths, it makes me sick.'

'Mice have chewed through meters of electrical wiring, in the process destroying a new stove, a fridge, a freezer and even a television set.'

'When you lie in bed at night you feel them run across your face. Fair dinkum, it drives you crazy . . . the stench from droppings and dead mice was almost overpowering at times.'

Even with mice in these unimaginable numbers, it appears they did not play a role in the transmissions of human diseases. A few cases of salmonellosis occurred, as did some cases of dermatomycoses due to a mite found only in Australia.

There are many ways to control mice, but some of the most interesting occurred when the ancient Greeks had a mouse problem. They believed mice could read and had a standard warning they would post near mouse infestations: "I adjure ye, ye mice here present, that ye neither injure me nor suffer another mouse to do so. I give you yonder field [usually some neighbor's property] but if I catch you here again, by the Mother of God, I will rend you in seven pieces." The eviction notice was stuck under a stone in the field, making sure the written side was facing up.

Apparently not only Greeks wrote messages to rodents. In Sandwich, New Hampshire, a note dated May 9, 1845, was found in the crevice of an old basement. The note read:

"I have bourn with you till my patience is gone. I cannot find words bad enough to express how I feel . . . now spirits of the bottomless pit, depart from this place with all speed! Begone our you are ruined. . . . We are preparing water (to) drown you; fire to roast you; cats to catch you; and clubs to maul you. . . . This is for cellar rats. Please give this notice to these in the chamber. There are many of us plotting against you. . . ."

E. Topsell, in his book *The Historie of Foure-Footed Beastes*, published in 1607, said that if mice were left in a pot without water they would kill one another. The winner, if turned loose, would hunt down and eat other mice. In the early 1800s Norwegians singed the hair of a rat over a fire and let it loose. The smell was so offensive to his comrades that they quitted the house.

Before we explore more conventional ways to control mice, let's discuss just how "dangerous" they are. Rodents worldwide are known to be responsible for close to sixty diseases, some with very intimidating names such as bunyaviral fever, boutonneuse fever, tsutsugamushi disease, leptospirosis, leishmaniasis, and angiostronglyiasis. The majority of these diseases are spread by rodents other than house mice and are more prevalent in third world countries. Hantavirus is a debilitating and potentially dangerous disease spread by deer mice and cotton rats, but not by house mice.

There are four basic types of rodent-borne diseases. They are viral zoonoses, rickettsial diseases, bacterial diseases, and parasitic zoonoses. These various diseases are spread by one of three ways: contamination from rodent urine and feces; rodent bites and arthropod vectors, usually fleas; and mites and ticks.

Diseases attributed to house mice are as follows:

Viral Zoonoses

Haemorrhagic Fever with Renal Syndrome (HFRS)
Large quantities of the virus are excreted in the urine, saliva, and feces of infected mice. This disease, however, is a problem in Asia and is not found in this country.

Lymphocytic Choriomeningitis (LCM)
Cases of human disease resulting from mice infected with LCM are rare. There have only been 239 human cases between 1960 and 1988, and all of them have been attributed to the Syrian hamster in laboratories, although the house mouse can be a reservoir. It is spread by food and water contaminated by rodent feces and urine.

Rickettsial Diseases

Rickettsialpox
This disease is spread by a mouse mite (*Allodermanysus sanguineus*). There were five hundred cases between 1946 and 1949

in New York City. The disease has been reported in a few other urban centers.

Murine Typhus

This is a flea-borne disease spread by fleas common to rats. One flea, the house mouse flea (*Leptopsylla segnis*), is suspected of transmitting murine typhus, but that has not been substantiated.

Bacterial Diseases

Leptospirosis

This widespread disease is spread by contact with infected animals, water, moist soil, and vegetation contaminated with urine or feces. Occupations most susceptible to leptospirosis are rice and sugar cane workers, farmers, miners, dairy workers, fishermen, and military personnel in the field.

Salmonellosis

Transmission is usually through the ingestion of food or water contaminated with urine or feces. This is a very common disease that has many causative agents. House mouse contamination is not common, but possible.

Parasitic Zoonoses

Toxoplasmosis

This is a protozoal infection generally transmitted by cats. The protozoan has been found in house mice in California.

There are a number of ways to control mice, although some of them are not desirable in our opinion. We never recommend rodenticides for several reasons. First, it is an inhumane way to kill mice or rats. If the rodent has to be killed, then a typical snap trap baited with candy (Tootsie Roll, gum drop, Hershey, etc.) will catch most mice. We prefer to catch mice using curiosity traps as illustrated below. You put the trap along the wall and bait it with oatmeal. The mouse will go in and not be able to get out. The trap will hold six or eight mice comfortably. We then release the mice away from the building where they are a nuisance.

Another method, which is taboo in my opinion, is the use of glue boards for mice. Nothing is more pitiful than watching a mouse struggle for its life while stuck in a glue board. I have had homeowners call me and complain that their pest control company put out glue boards, and the mice were caught and suffered for three or more days before dying from exhaustion. Pest control does not have to be barbaric in order to be successful. The curiosity traps (Tin Cats, Repeaters) are the best method available to catch mice.

- In a month a mouse will eat about five ounces of food and produce 1,500 droppings. (I bet someone got some taxpayer money to come to this conclusion).
- Mice can jump down ten feet without injury, leap up twelve inches, walk along a telephone line, swim (but don't like to),

A humane mousetrap. The best way to catch mice. This mouse was released right after I took the picture.

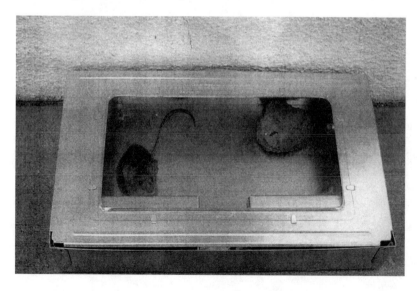

are color blind, and have poor vision, but have an excellent sense of smell.

- In 1926 in central California, the field mouse population exploded to the point that it was estimated there were 82,000 mice per acre.

16. TERMITES

Termite Misidentificaton (from Carl Olson)

I got a call from a man here in Tucson who wanted some insects identified. A year or so ago he had termite tube in a wall in his garage so he contacted a PCO and they sold him on a baiting system, the savior of us all. They installed it and took his money, came back and checked like all good companies do, had little activity,

Subterranean Termites. Workers under a board in my yard.

and declared the colony eradicated. Well the technician returned probably last week, opened the traps, and discovered some strange insects inside and tentatively called them drywood termites. Since she wasn't positive she either took specimens or a description back to the office for confirmation. Sure enough, the office agreed, and called the man and informed him that he would need to have his house tented and fumigated immediately to prevent damage. Needless to say, this pretty much freaked him out, so he called me to ask my thoughts on the situation.

Now not only can we get subterranean termite elimination from baits, but we can also discover when drywood termites have invaded too using this wonderful technology. I am just so impressed I can't stand it. Unfortunately the man didn't have the specimens for me to look at but I told him next time to save them and bring them in. I want to learn all about this new strain of subterranean drywood termites that appear in October in the desert. Fascinating story.

Gassy Termite Story (from Cam Lay)

The guy with the termite rig called me to ask my opinion about pumping gasoline under slabs to dissolve Styrofoam insulation used in synthetic stucco. Even though he was one of our worst PCOs in the state (we used to call his shop "the hog farm" because of the terrible piles of unwashed containers and just plain trash that littered the whole property), I didn't have the heart to tell him, "Yeah, man. Sounds good to me. Go for it." Plus, I figured that the fireball resulting from 100 gallons of gasoline in the termite rig might take out the whole neighborhood.

While crawling under a house in Miami looking for termites, my flashlight completely died out. As I had made several turns in the crawlspace, I could no longer see the opening or daylight. I started crawling toward where I thought the opening was when I heard a low growl. Never having heard that noise before, I thought a dog was under the house with me. I fished out my cigarette lighter (thank God I smoked in those days!) and lit it, only to find I had almost crawled over a six-foot alligator that was sleeping under the house. Needless to say I crawled in the dark (I dropped my lighter) as fast as I could in the opposite direction. It took me only a few minutes to see the opening and I got to it on my stomach lickety-split. Apparently the alligator couldn't be bothered with my intrusion, as he never moved. I reported to the lady that there was no evidence of termites but that she had an alligator infestation under the home. She knew the thing was living under there but had forgotten to tell me.

Termites are social insects that are more closely related to cockroaches than they are to ants, though they are often referred to as "white ants." Termites are an important part of the ecosystem, returning nutrients from dead trees to the soil to be reused. Unfortunately termites cannot distinguish between dead trees and the walls of your home.

Termites will not only eat the walls of your home but will destroy paper products, furniture, stored food, and any substance that contains cellulose. In fact, much information about early human history in South America and the tropics has been lost due to the paper-eating habits of termites. In this country, termites cause more damage annually than all the hurricanes, tornadoes, and fires combined.

Of the five major groups of termites found in this country, two are serious pests in homes. These are subterranean termites and drywood termites. Subterranean termites are found throughout much of the United States, whereas drywood termites are restricted to the extreme southern portion of the country, being common in Florida and California.

Subterranean termite colonies contain several castes, each with specific functions. A typical colony consists of a queen, numerous secondary reproductives that take over the egg-laying duties if the queen dies, soldiers, workers, nymphs, and alates, or winged reproductives. A single colony can contain over one million termites. Subterranean termites must have direct contact with the soil in order to survive. Drywood termites attack wood directly and do not have contact with the soil. Their colonies are much smaller, but there can be several colonies in a home, causing widespread damage. It is very difficult to control drywood termites without professional help. One option would be to treat all exposed wood with a borate product such as BoraCare or TimBor. This would help prevent an infestation but would not eradicate an existing one.

To help prevent subterranean termite infestation, a homeowner can install effective baiting systems him or herself. These systems can be useful in areas where there is high termite activity. If you suspect you already have subterranean termites, you will probably want to hire a professional. When you hire someone, make sure he or she is licensed and insured. If the person can't provide proof of insurance or a state license, call someone else. Make sure the termite technician makes a graph of your home showing what, if anything, they find while doing an inspection. The graph will also detail how they intend to treat the structure and how much termiticide they will use. You should also examine the guarantee to make sure he or she will come back if the termites come back. We don't recommend going with the low bid when contemplating a termite treatment, as you will get exactly what you pay for.

If the termite company is going to use a baiting system, you should ask the same questions, then decide if you want to pay someone to do this or do it yourself. Doing your own termite control using a bait system isn't hard for the average person, but there can be some complications to take into consideration, such as drilling adjoining patios and installing bait stations in the slab.

Installing termite baiting systems is not rocket science and can be accomplished by almost anyone. Most baiting systems contain monitoring stakes and treated stakes. The brand I use and recommend is FirstLine, and I will refer to it in this section. You should bury the monitoring stakes around the house in strategic places, putting more stakes in areas where termites are more likely to be found, such as near areas of excessive moisture or where wood touches the ground. If you have a crawl space, you should install them both in the crawl space along the foundation and near the support piers, as well as around the outside of the home. If you have a patio or sidewalk next to the house, you can use a jackhammer drill to drill a hole large enough for the stake to go through, and insert the monitoring stake right through the patio. FirstLine comes with a flat top on the bait station so it is easy to see and not unattractive to look at. The stakes should be placed next to the house, about a foot from the foundation. They can be ten or fifteen feet apart, but it is more important to place them in areas conducive to termites than to use a set distance between the stakes.

Once installed, they should be checked every four or five weeks. If you find activity, remove the monitoring stake and install a treated stake. The termites will take the bait and bring it back to their colony, thereby eradicating it. If you have an active infestation of subterranean termites (the baiting system doesn't work for drywood termites), the system may not eradicate the termites on its own. When termites are entrenched in your house, they may not spend the necessary energy and calories looking for a new food source if they have a perfectly good house to eat. The purpose of a termite baiting system is to prevent termites from getting into the house, not eradicating them once they are already in. I always suggest in this case that you have the home spot treated by a pest control company in the areas where there is termite activity, and then you can install the baiting system. Don't let them use a termiticide around the perimeter of the house or it will negate the efficacy of the termite bait you install later. Some commercial brands used by pest control operators claim to eradicate termites without any pesticides. What they don't tell you is that it may take years for the bait to be effective.

Final Note—If you have swarming termites in your home, there is no reason to waste them. Here is a recipe:

1 pint termite swarmers
1 tablespoon vegetable oil
$^1/_2$ teaspoon salt
Remove the wings from the termites and let the termites dry out. Put vegetable oil in a pan and spread dried termites on it. Heat until almost crisp. Sprinkle with salt. Eat like popcorn immediately or store for future use—they can be stored for months.

17. BELIEVE IT OR NOT BUG FACTS

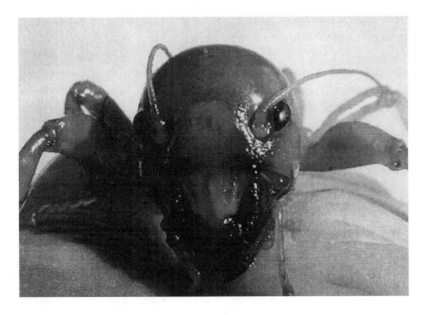

The Jerusalem cricket shown below is one of the most maligned insects in this country and for no good reason. Some Native Americans believe it is venomous, but it is nothing more than a harmless species of cricket. A large individual can deliver a painful

Child-of-the-Earth or Jerusalem Cricket, a.k.a., who-she-tsinni ("Old man bald head" in Navajo).

pinch that should be evident by looking at its mandibles, but they are not venomous.

According to legend, in 1848 hordes of insects began a feeding frenzy on the crops of early Mormon pioneers in Utah. They were so bad that the settlers prayed for help. After their prayer, hordes of seagulls suddenly appeared and devoured enough of the crickets to save the Mormons' crops. The insects have since been named Mormon crickets, and the Mormons built a statue of a seagull, which is still present in Salt Lake City, in honor of the bird that saved their crop. As far as we know, this is the only case of a statue being erected of a bird for eating bugs.

Also in Salt Lake City, a structure on the roof of a house resembles a huge beehive. This historic place was once the residence of Brigham Young, founder of the Mormon settlement, and is known as the "Beehive House."

In New Zealand a local cricket called a weta is four inches long and weighs three times as much as a mouse.

Insects that sing usually do so with their wings or legs, but some species of moths have singing penises. Male moths equipped with a singing penis perch with their genitals exposed to project their unique song. These singing sex organs are able to produce nearly pure tone ultrasonic signals.

During the War of 1812, a British warship sailed up the Patuxent River in Maryland. The officers went ashore to explore the countryside. When they noticed a hornet nest, they asked a young boy what it was because they were not familiar with it. The boy told them it was a rare hummingbird nest and if they plugged up the hole, took it aboard their ship, and unplugged the hole, the hummingbirds would fly around the ship all the way back to England. The officers followed the lad's advice, plugged the hole, and took the nest aboard their vessel, where they unplugged the hole. Shortly after that, people on shore watching through looking glasses saw the entire crew jump overboard as the irate hornets attacked everyone in sight. A verse by Robert Hinman tells the story:

> *The hornets surely won the day,*
> *And made their foes feel shame;*
> *These insects were American,*
> *And lived up to their name!*

A large sphinx moth, known as the "Death's Head," was made famous in the movie *Silence of the Lambs*. This moth has a marking on its back that resembles a skull and crossbones. Furthermore, these moths make a squeaking noise that the superstitious associate with the anguished moaning of a child. They regard it as an omen of coming evil or imminent death. It was a good choice for the movie.

The following poem is by Bill Holm from his book, *Boxelder Bugs Variations*, published by Milkweed Press. This book is devoted to boxelder bugs, a common pest in many parts of the country. Bill's book puts boxelder bugs in a positive light.

In a house with boxelder bugs
you're never lonely;
quiet neighbors who
leave whiskey alone,
don't wake you at night
with drunk stories of old
girlfriends, lives
gone wrong, new poems.
Boxelder bugs don't pay
much attention to whether
you get your work done.

As it says in pamphlets'
from various churches
and helping professions,
they are just there
whenever they are needed,
whether they are wanted,
just there

And there   And there
And there   And there   And there

And there   And there   And there
And there

The Rocky Mountain locust caused considerable damage in the Midwest during the 1800s. The Missouri State Legislature even put a bounty on them. Below is a firsthand account of the damage they can do as written in the *Salinas County*, Kansas's newspaper in September 1876:

Dear Father. No man can successfully fight against nature. The contest is unequal—nature caring no more for a man than for a grasshopper. Ah! the "hopper." Today, I lost sixty

INDEX

acres of wheat, eaten into the ground in less than an hour. I thought I had seen locusts two years ago, but I was mistaken. At about ten o'clock this morning, I noticed a heavy smoke rising in the West. I said to myself, "this is strange looking smoke. What causes it?" Rapidly it arose, smoke rising to the south, to the north, to the northeast. In a few minutes the column of smoke extended from the south around by the west to the northeast—to the extreme limit of vision. While I was saying to myself, "Yes, I understand you now," my heart slowly sank. Unhitching my team, I put my fall wheat sacks in the wagon, hitched to it, and drove to the granary, unloaded, drove to the house, got my gun and went prairie chicken shooting. Soon the low hum, as of a distant threshing machine, filled the air—the advance of the locusts. Louder, louder, even louder the hum, till in a roar the countless billions of devourers were on us, all around us. The air was stiff with them. I could look at the sun without blinking. They settled constantly. The earth was covered with them, yet not one in a thousand stopped. To the east they went in a vast cloud. A west wind, a gale, blew them. For six hours, they flew, a solid cloud; and tonight there is not a wheat plant left in any of the counties about here. I sat on a hill and watched them, and smiled as I saw hundreds tackle a sunflower, and laughed as I saw that sunflower vanish. How thick they were! How harmless they looked, but great Jove, how they ate! Ah! what appetites they have. It would make a dyspeptic turn green with envy see the way they fasten to anything and everything edible. The characteristic of a grasshopper's appetite is that all he eats runs to appetite. Sixty acres of my wheat was up. Now it is down—the gullets of the locusts. I have joy in saying that I have 80 acres of corn that will try their teeth somewhat. It is as hard as corn can be. I walked down this afternoon to see how they were making out with it. They had the stalks all stripped of leaves and were sawing at the corn. But I could see that it was no go. Their teeth

slipped over the bright yellow surfa
fectly cleared; beans, cabbages, tom
thing utterly gone. The vines to the
I am expecting a boss hopper up h
request the loan of a spade to dig up m
refuse his request with scorn.

odorous house ants, **56**
"old man bald head." *See* Jerusalem
crickets
Olson, Carl, 21–22, 114–15
orchard mason bees, 23
organophosphates, 24
Oriental cockroaches, 46, 50
Oriental rat flea, 97

palmetto bugs. *See* American
cockroaches
pantry pests, 47, 90–92; spreading
diseases, 90
Paratrechina longicornis (crazy ant), **59**
pavement ants, 64, **65**
Periplaneta americana (American
cockroach), 1, 46, **49**
pest control: glue boards, 47, 86, 88,
112; pesticides as a last resort, 36;
with predators, 92, 120; by
prevention, 17, 35–36; quick chart
for, 46–47; by removal, 16, 47, 85,
95; sanitation, 36, 44, 47, 70;
shampoos, 47, 103; soap and water,
17, 58, 60, 75, 107. *See also* baits;
Integrated Pest Management
(IPM); traps
pest control companies, 1; how to hire,
44–46; lawsuits against, 22, 100;
misidentification of pests, 35, 93,
100, 114–15; misuse of pesticides,
17–27, 36–38, 40, 53–54; "spray
and pray" methods, 17–19, 36–38;
training of employees, 32
pest control operators. *See* pest control
companies
pesticide labels, 26–27, 46; active
ingredients, 28; "Caution," 28;
"Danger," 28; "For Profession Use
Only," 27; "Hazards to Humans,"
29; inert ingredients, 28–29;
"Poison," 28; "Restricted Use
Pesticide," 27; "Warning," 28. *See
also* Material Safety Data Sheets
(MSDS)
pest prevention check list, 43–44

pesticides, ix; 18–20, aerial application
of, 22–23; banning of, 23–24;
indoor residues, 24; as a last resort,
36; misuse of, 17–27, 36–38, 40,
53–54; spot application of, 37
pests: conditions favoring, 4; facts
about, 107, 119–24; fear of, 5–9;
identification of, 17, 19, 35–36, 93,
100, 114–15
pets: Emperor scorpions, 89; food
storage, 44; Madagascan hissing
cockroaches, 51–52; and misuse of
pesticides, 21–22; nontoxic flea
collars, 98
pharaoh ants, **61**
Pheidole spp. (big-headed ant), **64**
pheromone traps, 37, 46–47, 51, 94
phobias, 5–9
Pholcidae (cellar spider family), 81–82
Phoridae (hump-back fly family), 68,
71
Phthirus pubis (crab louse), **101**
pillbug spiders, 82, **83**
Piophilidae (cheese skipper family), 71,
72
PIRG (Public Interest Research
Group), 42
plague: bubonic, 97; pneumonic,
97–98; septicemic, 97; sylvatic,
97–98
plague bacillus, 96–97
playground equipment, pest prevention,
43
Plodia interpunctella (Indian meal
moth), **91**, 94
pneumonic plague, 97–98
"Poison" on pesticide labels, 28
pollination, 23
pomace flies. *See* fruit flies
*Proceedings, Association of Avian
Veterinarians*, 22
Psychodidae (moth fly family), 68, **69**,
71
Public Interest Research Group
(PIRG), 42
pumpkin spiders, 84, **85**
pyramid ants, **57**, 58
pyrethrum, 1, 95